ANNETTE TROMLY

The Cover of the Mask: The Autobiographers in Charlotte Brontë's Fiction

ELS EDITIONS

ELS Editions
Department of English
University of Victoria
Victoria, BC
Canada V8W 3W1
www.elseditions.com

Founding Editor: Samuel L. Macey

General Editor: Luke Carson

Printed by CreateSpace

English literary studies monograph series
ISSN 0829-7681 ; 26
ISBN-10 0-920604-05-6
ISBN-13 978-0-920604-05-2

For My Mother

CONTENTS

ACKNOWLEDGEMENTS

I am grateful to a number of people for their assistance with this project: to Professor Samuel L. Macey, General Editor of the ELS Monograph Series, for his indulgence and co-operation; to my colleagues at Trent University's Academic Skills Centre and at Traill College—Isabel Henniger, Lynn Neufeld, Nancy Sherouse, and Peter Slade—for help with many arrangements; to Gay Marsden and Dianne Thompson, who typed the manuscript; to Jackie Todd, who removed obstacles at important times; to my sons, Luke and Ben, who were patient and encouraging; and to my friend Sheldon Zitner, whose devoted harassment kept me at my task. I am deeply indebted to Professor Fred Flahiff of St. Michael's College, University of Toronto, for the unstinting generosity with which he has shared his knowledge of Charlotte Brontë; a number of the ideas in my study had their genesis in our discussions. Professor Flahiff's contagious respect for the integrity of Charlotte Brontë's art is, I hope, reflected in my treatment of the novels. To my husband, Fred Tromly, mere thanks would be ingratitude.

ANNETTE TROMLY

Peterborough, Ontario
January 1982

CHAPTER ONE

The Cover of the Mask

I

When my children were very young, when, as far as I can remember, the oldest was about ten years of age, and the youngest about four, thinking that they knew more than I had yet discovered, in order to make them speak with less timidity, I deemed that if they were put under a sort of cover I might gain my end; and happening to have a mask in the house, I told them all to stand and speak boldly from under the cover of the mask.—PATRICK BRONTE[1]

It is tempting to read this wonderfully evocative scene in metaphorical terms, and to see in it the genesis of the Brontë children's art. As Charlotte and her siblings learn to "speak boldly from under the cover of the mask," we can imagine them adopting the personae which make fictional discourse possible. And for Charlotte, who later created three first-person narrators in her novels, Mr. Brontë's experiment with masks would seem to have borne especially rich fruit.

But if we read the scene with an awareness of the critical tradition which has surrounded Charlotte's novels, we may find in it a more disconcerting symbolic import. The scene provides a misleading paradigm for understanding Brontë's fiction because it fails to account for the complex transformation of personality into art. Charlotte's father assumed that the donning of a mask would allow his child to disclose the contents of her mind and heart for his inspection; too many critics have read her novels with the same assumption. Indeed, much of the commentary on the novels reads as if it were written by an adult who has just watched an awkward child living out her fantasies and crying out her pain behind a naïvely thin disguise. What is lacking in much Brontë criticism is a willingness to read the novels as coherent fictions without recourse to what we know (or think we know) of their creator—without the familiar threadbare backdrop of Haworth, without the presence of Charlotte's notorious family, and, most important, without our usual expectations of a child behind the mask. A careful reading of the first-person narratives will, I think, reveal an artist who is quite different from the Charlotte we have come to expect: formidable, mature, and very much in control of the mask through which she speaks.

If a single issue has bedevilled Brontë studies, it has been the problematic relation between the person and the mask—the extent to which we can read the novels from the evidence of the life, and the extent to which we can discern an autobiographical voice in the fiction. Victorian and early modern criticism tended to emphasize the person, sometimes to the total neglect or even denial of the fiction. Thus Leslie Stephen's solution offered an enviable lack of complexity by declaring that "the study of her life is the study of her novels":

> The most obvious of all remarks about Miss Brontë is the close connec-
> tion between her life and her writings. In no books is the author more
> completely incarnated. She is the heroine of her two most powerful novels.
> ... All the minor characters, with scarcely an exception, are simply por-
> traits, and the more successful in proportion to their fidelity. The scenery
> and even the incidents are, for the most part, equally direct transcripts
> from reality.[2]

Few modern critics would endorse Stephen's crudely reductive identification of the life and art. In fact, one strand of recent commentary has expressed a healthy skepticism about what has been called "the Purple Heather School of Criticism and Biography."[3] Yet even these studies have not always been content to read the fiction as art.[4] Our firmly fixed conception of the kind of person we assume Brontë to have been has usually led us to set fairly narrow limits around the statements we allow ourselves to make about the novels. But this is not surprising. Even the most cautious reader may find it difficult to let the novels stand free from a life which looms so large.

The recent trend toward psychobiographical criticism represents a variation —albeit a highly stimulating and inventive one—on Leslie Stephen's position. Rather than identifying the people and places in the novels with counter-parts in Brontë's life, these critics suggest that both the life and the work are reactions to some early psychic need or deprivation that Brontë experienced.[5] Although the portraits of Brontë herself which psychobiographers posit are of considerably more depth than the traditional one, they are also highly speculative. And more speculative yet are the readings of the novels which are predicated on these portraits. Like Leslie Stephen, psychobiographical critics tend to give emphasis to the presence of the suffering Charlotte behind the mask. Moreover, their approach continues to deny Brontë's work the dignity of consciously shaped art.

Another way in which recent criticism has redirected, rather than aban-doned, the biographical approach is by concerning itself with Brontë's ideas. Rejecting the landmarks of Charlotte's life, many commentators—like the father examining the masked child—have searched instead for the landmarks of her thought. Instead of canvassing the novels for undigested traces of Brontë's experience, they have tended to mine them for expressions of her opinion. As a result, twentieth-century studies of Brontë's religious beliefs, her social values, and her position as a feminist sometimes perpetuate, in a different idiom, early biographical studies.[6] One method errs by reducing "the House of Fiction to a home full of scrapbooks and family albums";[7] the other risks translating these Brontë scrapbooks into mere collections of essays. Behind the old approach stood Brontë the morbid sufferer (to whom Leslie Stephen continually condescended); but behind the new stands, all too often, Brontë the doctrinaire thinker—the apologist for the narrow moral positions held by the heroines of the novels. Thus Jane Eyre's decision to temper her passion with reason is confused with Brontë's purpose in writing the novel. What is on the surface of the novels—on the level of statement— is frequently equated with Brontë's artistic intentions. As Brontë the apologist replaces Brontë the sufferer, then, Brontë the creator continues to elude us.

Reconstructing Brontë's life and thought from inside her novels has not been successful, but reconstructing them from outside the works is not likely to be any more so. An attempt to rely on what we know of Charlotte as a key to understanding the novels is seriously jeopardized by the unreliability and paucity of the available historical materials. A notable case in point is the first, and most influential, biography. Shortly after her death, Brontë— the writer of fiction—was herself fictionalized by a novelist who had been asked to become a biographer. In the pages of Mrs. Gaskell's *The Life of Charlotte Brontë*, Charlotte became a conventional Victorian heroine, living a life of unrelieved anguish and self-denial. When Charles Kingsley praised the book by calling it "the picture of a valiant woman made perfect by suffering,"[8] he inadvertently revealed its limits as biography. Although it is now recognized that the portrait is as much an expression of Mrs. Gaskell as a depiction of Charlotte, this moving account, in varying degrees of explicitness, continues to underlie many discussions of Brontë's work.[9] The weakness of the early biographical foundation, however, should make us leery of attempting to discover Charlotte's autobiographical voice in the novels. We cannot be certain that we know her.

The unreliable portrait of Brontë which was bequeathed to us by her first biographer finds its counterpart in the equally unreliable status of the Brontë letters. We know that Charlotte's friend Ellen Nussey, to whom the bulk of the correspondence was written, tampered extensively with the let- ters—she edited, deleted, and destroyed. In addition, much of the correspon- dence had a labyrinthine history after it was wrested from both Ellen Nussey and Arthur Bell Nicholls by the unscrupulous T. J. Wise and his colleagues.[10] Correspondence that has been so deliberately adulterated, poorly edited, and hopelessly scattered is not to be depended upon to provide a reliable conception of the kind of person or artist Charlotte Brontë might have been.

Despite the unreliability of the records about Brontë, there are a few biographical observations that can be made with some degree of certainty. One of them, ironically enough, is that Charlotte was obsessed with privacy. Although it has been underemphasized by biographical critics both early and late, her desire to maintain her privacy is clear. We know about her pseudonym. We know in fact that anonymity was so important to her that she even assumed (unnecessarily) a third name at one point in her determination to conceal herself.[11] We know that she did not reveal her authorship for years, even to three of the people who were closest to her.[12] We know that with one of these people (Ellen Nussey) her indignant denial of a literary identity was so extreme as to be almost gratuitous.[13] Finally, we know that her letters to a number of people are shot through with such concerns as the "advantage of being able to walk invisible"[14] and the "sheltering shadow of an incognito."[15] We must not assume that such a thoroughly private artist, who once wrote to Ellen of "things which we should neither of us wish to commit to paper"[16] would make the secrets of her mind and heart easily available to us in her fiction.

Brontë's need for privacy is obliquely apparent throughout the correspondence. The Charlotte of the letters is an extremely elusive being; she has many voices. The letters, in fact, can be said to present at least as many different Charlotte Brontës as there were correspondents. As we recognize a nervously playful Charlotte with George Smith, a literary Charlotte with W. S. Williams, a domestic Charlotte with Ellen (etc.), we would do well to be cautious in the conclusions we draw about this very complicated being. Even if the letters were more reliable as historical documents, their value as sources of speculation about Brontë would be tenuous. At best, we can turn to them—as this study occasionally does—for indirect corroboration of observations we have gleaned from more solid evidence elsewhere.

A more deliberate distancing on Brontë's part arose from what Sydney Dobell referred to as her "masquerade": her assumption of a literary pseudonym.[17] Currer Bell has been characterized as either a convenience or a means of psychic escape for Charlotte. In fact, though, there is some evidence both in the novels and in the correspondence that Brontë interposed Bell quite self-consciously between herself and her art. It is interesting to note, for instance, how frequently Bell becomes a separate personage—almost an alter ego—in the letters.[18] When Brontë assured Williams, after having been insulted by a critic, that what Charlotte Brontë "feels or has felt is not the question—it is Currer Bell who was insulted,"[19] we recognize her characteristic insistence on Bell's separate identity. As much as any of her fictional characters, Currer Bell seems to have existed for Brontë. As a critic has written, "The device of the pseudonym . . . serves to distinguish the woman who suffers from the man who creates, separating the private world of Charlotte Brontë from the external world and from the world of her own creation."[20] Charlotte worked hard to keep the private self apart from the artist. Considering both the intensity of her efforts and the intensity of our curiosity about her, it would seem that time has mocked her wishes with uncommon malice.

Even if the biographical record were fuller and more reliable, and even if Brontë herself had allowed us to know her better, there would be good reason to avoid the biography as a way of entering the fiction. And the problem with the biographical approach is not simply its discovery of traces of the life in the art; no one would want to deny that the local habitations, if not the names, of Brontë's experience are present in the novels. "There is always," as Yeats assured us, "a living face behind the mask."[21] What is at issue, however, is just what becomes of the raw materials of a life in the alembic of a creative imagination. To cite a familiar case in point, there is no reason to suppose that Zoraïde Reuter—even if she were based on the model of Madame Heger—must be entirely, or even predominantly, sinister. The process of aesthetic transformation is always highly mysterious. What we have are the givens of the work itself; all else—especially in the case of Brontë—is speculation.

What is most pernicious about criticism which relies on biography, however, is its tendency to deny that Brontë was a conscious and deliberate artist. Appropriately, the most eloquent refutation of Leslie Stephen's biographical determinism was written by that consummate artificer, Henry James:

> The personal position of the three sisters . . . had been marked . . . with so sharp an accent that this accent has become for us the very tone of their united production. It covers and supplants their matter, their spirit, their style, their talent, their taste; it embodies, really, the most complete intellectual muddle, if the term be not extravagant, ever achieved, on a literary question, by our wonderful public. . . . the fashion has been, in looking at the Brontës, so to confound the cause with the result that we cease to know, in the presence of such ecstasies, what we have hold of or what we are talking about. They represent, the ecstasies, the high-water mark of sentimental judgment.[22]

James's warning has not yet been adequately heeded: the temptation to confound the cause with the result still remains.

13

The many pitfalls involved in reading Brontë's fiction as though it were her autobiography may incline us to agree with the critic who remarked that "the works are not autobiography in any real sense at all."[23] But this formulation obscures a central concern of Brontë's novels, a concern which is the focus of my study. *The Professor, Jane Eyre,* and *Villette* can all be fruitfully examined as autobiography. Paradoxically, the same issue which has so obfuscated the artistry of Brontë's fiction can lead us straight back to the aesthetic centres of the novels. For the novels are not Brontë's autobiography cast in fictional form; they are fictions cast in what Brontë called "the autobiographic form."[24] William Crimsworth, Jane Eyre, and Lucy Snowe are fictional autobiographers, each of whom Brontë depicts constructing his own life story.

It is important to note that when she chose autobiography as a narrative strategy, Brontë was creating yet another device for distancing. In these three novels, she has an even more substantial presence than Currer Bell mediating between herself and her work: a fully-realized fictional autobiographer. The primary task of creating has been displaced away from Brontë, onto Bell, and finally onto the first-person narrators that he created. Only by reading the novels with their narrative complexity in mind can we appreciate the deliberate artistry of these thrice-told tales.

Although it might seem that a comparison of Brontë's three first-person narratives with contemporary autobiography would be a fruitful line of investigation, such a study would be of questionable relevance. The popularity of the genre of autobiography in Brontë's time is well-known,[25] and we can safely say that Brontë shared in the nineteenth-century interest in the genre.[26] But contemporary autobiographies do not provide a defining context for her fictional autobiographies. As Jane Eyre knew, these are not "regular" autobiographies, but novels. At best, regular autobiographies can perhaps provide analogues to the way in which Brontë's narrators addressed their task—but not to the way in which Brontë addressed hers. Brontë the novelist employed the narrative framework of autobiography as a means by which to explore an issue which was not narrowly generic: the motives, principles, and practices of self-presentation.

What we find in all three of these fictional autobiographies is the importance of the process of self-portraiture: the constant presence of the narrator actively shaping his story. Through necessarily oblique means, the novels invite us to see the narrators quite differently from the way these narrators see themselves.[27] A recent comment about *Villette* applies with equal force to the two other fictional autobiographies: "To see beyond the supposedly imperturbable, opaque surface of Lucy's story is the reader's most challenging responsibility."[28] Brontë's fictional autobiographies presage a number of modern attitudes toward self-presentation, among them that the psychological motivation behind writing a life of oneself is complicated, that autobiography distorts the truth (or creates its own), and that the faculty of memory is basically untrustworthy.[29] Indeed, a comment that André Maurois made some seventy-five years after Brontë's death speaks to a central concern of her novels:

> Memory is a great artist. For every man and for every woman it makes the recollection of his or her life a work of art and an unfaithful record.[30]

And from this attitude it is but a short step to the solidly post-Freudian concerns of critics such as Ernst Kris,[31] who writes about his clinical observations of the "autobiographical screen"[32] erected by patients:

> In all those areas where the self is concerned, where memory is autobiographical, autonomy in the broadest sense is never fully achieved, distorting influences never cease to play their part, and recollections remain connected with needs and affects.[33]

Long before either of these observations was made, Charlotte Brontë—through the agency of William Crimsworth, Jane Eyre, and Lucy Snowe—was exploring the potential distortions of self-portraiture. She too was aware that

> all people have their dark side—though some possess the power of throwing a fair veil over the defects; close acquaintance slowly removes the screen, and one by one the blots appear, till at length we sometimes see the pattern of perfection all slurred over with blots....[34]

Brontë's narrators create personal mythologies about themselves, mythologies which in their view endow their lives with heightened moral significance. In their accounts of their past—of the choices they made, the priorities they established, the wrongs they perceived—they often present to us, to use Charlotte's terms, "pattern[s] of perfection," with all the blots veiled. In claiming this heightened moral significance, the narrators elevate their quotidian pursuits; they present themselves as prototypes for the revelation of human meaning. Constructing their lives in terms of the moral growth of their characters, they adumbrate a main theme in nineteenth-century commentary on autobiography. John Foster's popular essay (first published in 1805 and reprinted numerous times during the century) entitled "On a Man's Writing Memoirs of Himself,"[35] claimed that the serious autobiographer should be

15

"endeavoring not so much to enumerate the mere facts and events of life, as to discriminate the successive states of the mind, and the progress of character."[36] In their accounts of their lives, Brontë's three narrators would seem to be striving to construct patterns of the moral "progress of character" that Foster suggests. Thus William Crimsworth presents his life as a latter-day Pilgrim's Progress;[37] his success story involves overcoming a series of moral obstacles in order to obtain both happiness and prosperity. Thus Lucy Snowe creates a series of deaths and rebirths for herself in order to illustrate the forward motion of her story. And thus Jane Eyre portrays her married life at Ferndean as a hard-won compromise between impossible alternatives.

William Crimsworth, Jane Eyre, and Lucy Snowe, then, all organize their experience into patterns of moral progress which inflate the claims of the individual history. Patterns, however, also simplify. All three personal mythologies reflect a pronounced constriction of outlook, a chosen containment by the autobiographer of what is irreducible in his life to the terms of a paradigm. Inevitably, these paradigms suffer from "leakage."[38] Presenting neatly finished portraits of themselves in the novels, the narrators are betrayed by the loose ends which Brontë dangles before the reader. Crimsworth's alleged domestic paradise is achieved at the expense of his wife and son. Jane Eyre's presumed amalgamation of nature and grace in the last chapter transpires in a mephitic atmosphere. Lucy's relief at the departure of the man she loves undercuts her professions of martyrdom when his journey proves fatal. Brontë's narrators ultimately betray the inadequacy of their autobiographical perceptions.

All of Brontë's narrators complacently embrace formulaic modes of thought about themselves and their worlds. The limitations of the autobiographers' self-portraits (and portraits of others) are indicated in part by a pervasive network of enclosure imagery in the novels. Each of the three autobiographers is associated with a characteristic mode of enclosure—a physical image which points to his particular mode of mental confinement. Thus, Jane Eyre is often found in unlocked rooms; William Crimsworth needs to enclose things securely in small places; and Lucy Snowe contains her true nature within a disguise. And echoing the narrators' enclosures are many other images of confinement in the novels; houses, rooms, and walled gardens abound. These images have an inherently ironic function: they move in two directions at once.[39] For the narrators, they help to establish gratifying personal limits; they enhance a reassuring definition of the self. For the reader, however, the enclosures signify limitation; they indicate the narrator's need to circumscribe his experience. When William Crimsworth, for example, speaks of the people he meets as framed portraits, he uses the image smugly in order to contrast these people (pejoratively) with himself. For the reader, however, Crimsworth is simplifying and schematizing his world, reducing the complexity of other human beings. Similarly, Lucy Snowe feels protected in the walled garden of the school where she is employed; but we note that Lucy's need for such enclosures reflects her fear of the untidy real world. This simultaneous need of Brontë's first-person narrators to reduce their experience and to inflate themselves establishes the novels' dominant ironic mode.

From one perspective, Brontë's autobiographers are Everymen, characterized by the frailties which inevitably attend self-presentation. But from another perspective they illuminate a more particular concern—the artist's attempt to create a truthful image. All of Brontë's narrators possess artistic or imaginative sensibilities;[40] their stories re-create the process of artistic self-portraiture. All of the novels, then, are in one sense about the relation of an artist to his mask. Brontë found in fictional autobiography an appropriate narrative form through which to explore this relation. For it is a form which hovers on the border between public apology and private confession; it encompasses both truth and distortion. As we shall note, all of Brontë's autobiographers remain ambiguous in defining their narrative functions; they view themselves alternately as shaping artists or as "professedly truthful"[41] historians of their lives. It is clear that Brontë deliberately refrained from clarifying the role of her narrators. In allowing them to interfere with their stories (as novelists would) and at the same time to attest to the verisimilitude of their narratives, she was posing a crucial question about the nature of their art. That question centres on the validity of the self-image the autobiographers project in their stories.

Frequently, as we shall see, the autobiographers use aesthetic imagery to inflate their experience. Filtering their private perceptions through the language and figures of the arts, they claim a universal import for their personal lives. When Crimsworth speaks of his life as a gallery of paintings, for example, he imposes special meaning on a fairly mediocre existence. For Jane Eyre and Lucy Snowe, art is a more central concern. These autobiographers retreat into art as an alternative to addressing their lives forthrightly.

In her three first-person narratives, Brontë viewed dispassionately the issue of an artist's motivation, his honesty, his true relation to the portrait he projected. Throughout the books there is constant tension between the self-image as perceived by the autobiographer and the image of the self as perceived by the reader. Finally, the novels' ironies are gathered up in what becomes both the ultimate work of art and the ultimate enclosure for the narrators: the act of writing an autobiography itself. All three artists circumscribe by means of their stories; in defining themselves, they confine themselves. The creative act for Brontë's autobiographers is in the end an act of moral ambiguity, inseparable from self-delusion and the delusion of others. At the centre of Brontë's creative commitment is a fundamental ambivalence about the truth and morality of art.

The widely-held view of Charlotte Brontë as a moralist is not, therefore, incorrect. But it is a mistake to locate Brontë's moral beliefs by confusing them with the incidental *obiter dicta* of the fictional characters she creates. Insofar as we can ascertain Brontë's judgments, we must expect them to be implicit rather than explicit, related not so much to what the characters believe as to their motives for believing. We find Brontë's position, for instance, not so much in Jane Eyre's statements about reason and passion as in her need for unrealistic self-representation. Qualifying the portraits of all three autobiographers is Brontë's objection to the smug self-satisfaction of those who reduce the world to a set of easy certainties.

Brontë's interest in the presentation of character is reflected in her numerous comments on contemporary biographies.[42] The nineteenth century was as zealous about biography as it was about autobiography[43]—and Brontë shared in the enthusiasm of her day. But by the time she was writing her novels, the quality of the biography being written had slipped far below its quantity. As an historian of the genre explains, "For biography it was a regressive age marked by the return to popularity of the panegyric and the commemorative life. By the 'forties biography was rapidly descending into complete respectability."[44] Attempts to idealize the subjects of biographies with uncritical irresponsibility (to abandon, in other words, earlier Boswellian candour) annoyed the more substantial moralists of the age. As early as 1821, one critic complained that "biographical memoirs have become as multitudinous, prolix, and veracious as epitaphs in a country churchyard."[45] And Carlyle, an influential commentator on biography, lodged his own sardonic protest: "How delicate, how decent is English biography, bless its mealy mouth."[46]

Charlotte Brontë shared Carlyle's concern. An avid reader of lives, she objected when a biographer descended to gratuitous adulation of people she considered less than impressive. She felt that Mirabeau's biographer did not call adequate attention to his subject's mistakes:

It appears to me that the biographer errs also in being too solicitous to present his hero always in a striking point of view—too negligent of the exact truth. He eulogizes him too much; he subdues all the other characters mentioned and keeps them in the shade, that Mirabeau may stand out more conspicuously.[47]

18

Brontë's many comments on biography indicate a keen interest in the problem of how a life might be presented. Always ready to applaud a deserving subject for his moral substance,[48] she nevertheless reserved a considerable amount of skepticism for the excessively zealous portrait—the portrait which veiled the "dark side." As we might expect, this same insistence on candour informed Brontë's judgment of fictional autobiography. She criticized *Bleak House* because Esther Summerson's "history" (cast in what Brontë called "the autobiographic form") is "too often weak and twaddling; an amiable nature is caricatured, not faithfully rendered. . . ."[49]

Throughout her career, Brontë asserted her dedication to Truth:[50]

The first duty of an author is, I conceive, a faithful allegiance to Truth and Nature; his second, such a conscientious study of Art as shall enable him to interpret eloquently and effectively the oracles delivered by those two great deities.[51]

Although, as Earl A. Knies has demonstrated, Brontë's terminology is often vague,[52] it does seem apparent that the Truth she espouses is what she defines to Mrs. Gaskell as "severe Truth":

Does no luminous cloud ever come between you and the severe Truth as you know it in your own secret and clear-seeing soul? In a word, are you never tempted to make your characters more amiable than the Life, by the inclination to assimilate your thoughts to the thoughts of those who always *feel* kindly, but sometimes fail to *see* justly?[53]

In both theory and practice, Brontë rejected the merely amiable, the pleasantly idealized, the "luminous cloud," in favour of Truth. Her commitment in fiction was to the way things are, and not to the way things might be. As she wrote later to her publishers, "To shun examination into the dangerous and disagreeable seems to me cowardly."[54]

So conceived, Brontë's moralism may be called the cornerstone of her aesthetics. And her substantial creative gift coupled with her strong moral concern allows us to speak of her best in paradox. She created art by demonstrating how others abused it. She distanced herself from private experience by creating fictional artists who lacked that distance. She skeptically questioned the moral foundation of art even as she dedicated herself to creating. And, as the excellence of her novels will attest, her denial of art is itself an affirmation.

CHAPTER TWO

The Professor

From its earliest reviews onward, critics have accorded *The Professor* the same reception which greeted the return of Milton's Satan to Hell: "a dismal universal hiss." Only one voice has disturbed this reassuring critical certitude; and the dissenting voice has belonged to the person who is apparently least qualified to speak. Charlotte Brontë herself seems not to have faltered in her commitment to her first novel. She tried nine times to get *The Professor* published (it originally was rejected by six publishers), renewing her effort each time one of her other novels was more sympathetically received.[1] Brontë even attempted to use *Jane Eyre*'s popularity as a coat-tail by which her earlier narrative might be introduced to the reading public. Her efforts failed; it was not until after her death that George Smith decided to publish *The Professor*—only because he realized that nothing else was forthcoming.

Brontë described, in the "Biographical Notice of Ellis and Acton Bell," written for the 1850 edition of *Wuthering Heights, Agnes Grey*, and selected poems, her bitter disappointment at the book's reception: "Currer Bell's book found acceptance nowhere, nor any acknowledgement of merit, so that something like the chill of despair began to invade his heart."[2] The consensus that *Jane Eyre* was far superior to *The Professor* she took adamant exception to. The middle and latter portions of *The Professor*, she insisted, contained "more pith, more substance, more reality" than much of *Jane Eyre*.[3] But if Brontë's defence of *The Professor* was fervid, critics' attacks have been equally so. They have either disregarded Brontë's opinions, or, in one telling instance, denounced them. Referring to Brontë's statement about the novel's value, one critic has declared that the author is "in certain ways, as much of a hypocrite as William Crimsworth," the novel's narrator.[4]

Lying behind the animadversions against the book (in varying degrees of explicitness) are assumptions about its relation to Brontë's biography. First, critics have generally seen this maiden, unpublishable novel as a product of Brontë's artistic immaturity, the "work of a beginner."[5] (As a result, the need to make judgments about the novel—to locate signs of Brontë's apprenticeship—has too often taken precedence over the desire to understand it.) More specifically, some critics have seen the author as incompletely detached from her book, compromising its moral vision by her personal entanglements with the characters. Thus they believe that William Crimsworth, a "wholly decent young man,"[6] makes his way in a tough world by voicing directly the opinions of Charlotte Brontë.[7] Even those critics who have attempted to detach Crimsworth from Brontë (and have seen him as an essentially unreliable narrator) have not found credible artistic reasons for his limitations.[8] And similarly, Frances Henri has been seen as an idealized projection of Brontë herself.[9] Inevitably, most critics have fallen back on the shibboleth of Brontë's biography to dismiss what they consider to be *The Professor*'s shortcomings. Charlotte must have been, in the last year of correspondence with Heger, exorcising the frustrations of an unrequited love;[10] as a result, she wrote an uncontrolled novel.

No one would want to deny that traces of Charlotte Brontë's private world are present in the novel. In certain sections, particularly the chapters on Belgium, Brontë renders the raw materials of her own experience intensely. But if she appropriated certain materials from her life, she did not do so in any simple way. *The Professor* is not, above all, Brontë's unmediated autobiography. It is, however, William Crimsworth's autobiography. A careful examination of *The Professor* reveals a primary interest in the motives and processes of self-presentation; the book is informed by its exploration of the issue. By means of a thoroughly obtrusive and essentially unreliable narrative voice, Brontë explores the reasons and the ways that an autobiographer presents himself to the world. Decades after Brontë's death, Leslie Stephen observed that "distortions of the truth belong to the values of autobiography and are as revealing as the truth."[11] *The Professor* is a novel about these distortions.

The beginning of *The Professor* has always been an irritant to critics. William Crimsworth's letter to "Charles"—who neither answers the letter nor receives it, and does not appear again in the novel—certainly seems arbitrary and contrived. It is not surprising that one critic has called the letter a "clumsy piece of narrative technique."[12] Yet in being both clumsy and irritating, Crimsworth's letter, sent to nowhere, serves its purpose well. The reader does not get very far into the novel before he is forced to ask questions about the teller of the tale. What kind of person would begin his autobiography by quoting himself at length? Why does he adopt such a self-absorbed and callous tone to his old friend? Why does he write the unsolicited letter in the first place? Why is he clearly more interested in telling his story than in communicating with Charles? Surely Brontë is asking her reader, from the book's first moments, to be aware of the centrality of the narrative voice. William Crimsworth, writing from his study at Daisy Lane, is meant to be an emphatic presence.

Throughout the novel Brontë continues to obtrude Crimsworth onto the reader's attention; the narrator's handling of events continually calls attention to his shaping presence. In a number of instances Crimsworth, by means of brief or oblique allusions, passes over or underplays significant events in his life. Thus toward the end of the book he inserts the birth of his only son as an afterthought. Similarly, he downplays his rescue of Jean Baptiste Vandenhuten (who is introduced only as a means of explaining his progress in the search for employment), and skips completely his own professional experience throughout the years of his marriage. But perhaps the most tantalizing of these manipulations of significant events is his allusion to having once observed a "modern French novel":

> Now, modern French novels are not to my taste, either practically or theoretically. Limited as had yet been my experience of life, I had once had the opportunity of contemplating, near at hand, an example of the results produced by a course of interesting and romantic domestic treachery. No golden halo of fiction was about this example, I saw it bare and real, and it was very loathsome. I saw a mind degraded by the practice of mean subterfuge, by the habit of perfidious deception, and a body depraved by the infectious influence of the vice-polluted soul. I had suffered much from the forced and prolonged view of this spectacle; those sufferings I did not now regret, for their simple recollection acted as a most wholesome antidote to temptation.[13]

We hear no more of what must have been a formative experience for Crimsworth. His reticence about this and other matters points to a mind which is deliberately shaping its story. The reader is forced to wonder just what Crimsworth's principles of inclusion are.

If Crimsworth can de-emphasize the important experience, he can also inflate the unimportant. Under his pen the story of his life often unfolds as a series of significant inner moments struck into high relief largely by the force of his narrative determination. After leaving his job in Bigben Close, for example, he describes his walk into the country. He designates a fast-flowing river as his symbol-for-the-moment, and takes pains to impress it on both his memory and ours: "... I watched the rapid rush of its waves. I desired memory to take a clear and permanent impression of the scene, and treasure it for future years" (194). At other times the meanings Crimsworth imposes on his experience are more difficult to achieve. When he thinks he has lost Frances through the machinations of Zoraïde Reuter, he offers a long disquisition which begins with the proper sphere of the novelist, passes through the dangers of sensual indulgence, glances quickly at suffering, and finally alights on the consolation of Religion to the hopeless man (277-78). And all of this, he instructs the reader, so that we might infer that—being a reasonable man—he was able to control his grief. The sheer energy Crimsworth expends in imposing a rationale on his life suggests that we should be wary of sharing his perceptions.

Crimsworth's significant moments most often take the form of inner conflicts between moral abstractions. He regrets having resigned his teaching job, for example, when he realizes that he is not in a position to approach the now-employed Frances. But Conscience helpfully intervenes:

> "Down, stupid tormentors!" cried she; "the man has done his duty; you shall not bait him thus by thoughts of what might have been; he relinquished a temporary and contingent good to avoid a permanent and certain evil; he did well. Let him reflect now, and when your blinding dust and deafening hum subside, he will discover a path." (305)

Shortly afterward, on the night that he longs to give in to his desire to see Frances, Imagination is the "sweet temptress" which he manages to repel. There are many such moments in the novel. It is difficult to imagine that, had *The Professor* been illustrated,[14] Crimsworth would not have been represented with demons on one shoulder and angels on the other; his moral universe is thoroughly dichotomized.

Brontë presents her narrator, then, as the central problem of the novel. William Crimsworth the autobiographer is everywhere present, giving shape and emphasis to his story. And Crimsworth's autobiographical manipulations become morally questionable because of his pronounced tendency to self-inflation. The abstractions through which he filters his inner conflicts, for example, impart a self-serving suggestiveness to the events of his life. He elevates his personal significance by means of the patterns he imposes.

If, however, Crimsworth's version of his life gratifies the autobiographer, it suggests something quite different to the reader. What we note in Crimsworth's account—in his omissions, emphases, and interpretations of events—is its decided simplification of complexities. If Crimsworth expands his life's meaning in his own eyes, he contracts it in ours. His act of writing becomes an act of enclosure, an act of imposing a personal mythology upon a life. And through a network of images in the novel, Brontë further undercuts Crimsworth's self-portrait. Images of physical enclosure echo the mental enclosure which lies behind Crimsworth's autobiographical impulse.

I. Crimsworth: An Israelite in Brobdingnag

Fastidious, hypersensitive William Crimsworth (the name has a Dickensian aural appropriateness) expends a great deal of energy guarding himself against assault: assault by other people, assault by his own impulses, assault by all the untidy circumstances that disrupt a remarkably quotidian existence. Enclosure is his characteristic way of dealing with a world too threatening for his insecure psychic constitution. Crimsworth assumes a defensive self-protectiveness against most of his associates. He finds satisfaction in hiding his real self from his tyrannical brother's gaze: "... I felt as secure against his scrutiny as if I had had on a casque with the visor down ..." (176). Similarly, he handles his students with dispatch: "In less than five minutes they had thus revealed to me their characters, and in less than five minutes I had buckled on a breast-plate of steely indifference, and let down a visor of impassible austerity" (223). When uneasy, Crimsworth seeks places which are small and closed-in; after most events of consequence, he walks in "narrow chambers," or shuts out "intruders" (including, at times, the reader). By shutting himself up, or the world out, then, he manages to maintain a fragile state of equilibrium.

Just how fragile this state is, however, becomes most clear when the intruder is one of his own feelings. The scene mentioned earlier, in which he copes with his grief for the lost (misplaced) Frances, is a good example:

> being a steady, reasonable man, I did not allow the resentment, disappointment, and grief, engendered in my mind by this evil chance, to grow there to any monstrous size; nor did I allow them to monopolise the whole space of my heart; I pent them, on the contrary, in one strait and secret nook. In the daytime, too, when I was about my duties, I put them on the silent system; and it was only after I had closed the door of my chamber at night that I somewhat relaxed my severity towards these morose nurslings, and allowed vent to their language of murmurs; then, in revenge, they sat on my pillow, haunted my bed, and kept me awake with their long, midnight cry. (278)

Crimsworth's fear that without his "strait and secret nook" his feelings will grow monstrous is a consequence of his repression; the syndrome has become common coinage in the psychological currency of our day. And as familiar is the ironical result: the sheer act of forceful control defeats its own purpose. The feelings are unearthed in a more painful way—transformed to a morbid state. The strained, hyperbolical, frenzied language in which Crimsworth describes the revenge of his "morose nurslings" is apt. He is clearly so out of touch with his feelings that he can deal with them—and enjoy them

—only when they are dressed up in elaborate metaphor. Most of Crimsworth's psychic life can be characterized in terms of a similar tension: an excessive need for control along with its inevitable opposite.

Other enclosure images emphasize Crimsworth's unwholesome emotional obsessions. Sitting "alone near midnight" writing his autobiography at Daisy Lane, he attempts to capture his past. His memories rise before him like ghosts in a graveyard:[15]

> Belgium! I repeat the word, now as I sit alone near midnight. It stirs my world of the past like a summons to resurrection; the graves unclose, the dead are raised; thoughts, feelings, memories that slept, are seen by me ascending from the clods—haloed most of them—but while I gaze on their vapoury forms, and strive to ascertain definitely their outline, the sound which wakened them dies, and they sink, each and all, like a light wreath of mist, absorbed in the mould, recalled to urns, resealed in monuments. Farewell, luminous phantoms! (201)

As his griefs are pent in a "strait and secret nook," so his memories have been sealed in urns; both images represent a mind which immures the spacious potential of emotional experience. And in spite of this allusion to sinking phantoms, Crimsworth will never realize how thoroughly unsuccessful he is at resurrecting his past. As we shall see, his autobiography does not succeed in liberating his sealed memories; their forms will always remain indistinct to him.

As Crimsworth embalms his memories, so he enshrines his love:

> I loved the movement with which she confided her hand to my hand; I loved her as she stood there, penniless and parentless; for a sensualist charmless, for me a treasure—my best object of sympathy on earth, thinking such thoughts as I thought, feeling such feelings as I felt; my ideal of the shrine in which to seal my stores of love.... (285)

The woman he chooses is an "object" to contain his love; and he can describe his "ideal" only in terms of the gratifications she will provide for him. Crimsworth's brand of idealism, then, is as constricted as his repressed desires, his love enclosed as tightly as his grief and his memories. As we shall see, this strange person, whose thoughts are avowedly turned heavenward, becomes capable of the grimmest kind of mean-mindedness.

Crimsworth's tendency to enclose is so thoroughgoing that it undermines his perceptions altogether. He perceives his world as a series of pictures; his reliance on the visual arts is the most persistent peculiarity of his language. He consistently represents places (such as Belgium and the river in Grovetown mentioned above) as pictures. And virtually all the people he meets,

25

from an anonymous Flemish housemaid who reminds him of "the female figures in certain Dutch paintings" (202-03) to his good friend Yorke Hunsden, whose "features might have done well on canvas but indifferently in marble" (186) are subjected to the scrutinizing eye of a self-conscious artist. Crimsworth takes great pains when presenting his pictures; they are often overloaded with descriptive minutiae. His efforts at verisimilitude, however, reveal more about the artist than his subjects. Rather than rendering faithful images of the people he describes, Crimsworth avoids or distorts the issue of who they really are. Preoccupation with physical characteristics sometimes permits him to avoid more significant attributes of character. But more serious, perhaps, is his tendency to create simple equations between the outer person and the inner character. His student Eulalie is an example:

> Eulalie was tall, and very finely shaped: she was fair, and her features were those of a Low Country Madonna; many a 'figure de Vierge' have I seen in Dutch pictures exactly resembling hers; there were no angles in her shape or in her face, all was curve and roundness—neither thought, sentiment, nor passion disturbed by line or flush the equality of her pale, clear skin; her noble bust heaved with her regular breathing, her eyes moved a little—by these evidences of life alone could I have distinguished her from some large handsome figure moulded in wax. (222)

Crimsworth submits Eulalie to a process of reduction in several ways. First, by associating her with works of art he is able to distance himself from her. Second, in relying on the stock associations of a type of painted figure, he is forcing Eulalie into an easy and pre-existent category. And finally, the blandness of character he attributes to her on the basis of her physical type is predicated on a questionable relation between the inner and the outer person. Interpreting people as works of art enables Crimsworth to categorize his world far too neatly. Once enclosed in frames, his images become easier to control.

Crimsworth depicts himself as well as others. Even as the novel opens, he is speaking (in the letter to Charles) of his own "portrait." And in the most explicit summary he gives us of his past, his life becomes a gallery:

> Three—nay four—pictures line the four-walled cell where are stored for me the records of the past. First, Eton. All in that picture is in far perspective, receding, diminutive; but freshly coloured, green, dewy, with a spring sky, piled with glittering yet showery clouds; for my childhood was not all sunshine—it had its overcast, its cold, its stormy hours. Second, X——, huge, dingy, the canvas cracked and smoked; a yellow sky, sooty clouds; no sun, no azure; the verdure of the suburbs blighted and sullied—a very dreary scene.

Third, Belgium; and I will pause before this landscape. As to the fourth, a curtain covers it, which I may hereafter withdraw, or may not, as suits my convenience and capacity. At any rate, for the present it must hang undisturbed. (200)

In deliberately figuring his past as a gallery of pictures, Crimsworth, characteristically, claims an inflated meaning for his private experience. He presents his past, by analogy, as something that partakes of the heightened significance of paintings. Yet as he inflates, he also deflates. The frames around his past, like the urns that hold his memories, are enclosures. Even the gallery itself is a claustrophobic, four-walled cell. And Crimsworth chooses a curious kind of picture to represent his life. Each painting in the gallery might be titled "A Portrait of the Artist as a Young Landscape"; missing from the canvas is Crimsworth himself. Eulalie, then, is not the only figure who is dehumanized and regarded with detachment; Crimsworth also maintains a disturbing distance from himself. The mysterious fourth, curtained, picture is never alluded to again.[16] But as we shall see, despite Crimsworth's secrecy, it does not hang undisturbed.

From time to time Crimsworth reminds the reader that the pictures he is framing as he tells his story are corrected versions of the inaccurate pictures of his youth. An interesting dynamic develops as Crimsworth the Autobiographer, writing from Daisy Lane, enjoys contemplating his formerly callow perceptions:

This is Belgium, reader. Look! don't call the picture a flat or a dull one —it was neither flat nor dull to me when I first beheld it. When I left Ostend on a mild February morning, and found myself on the road to Brussels, nothing could look vapid to me. My sense of enjoyment possessed an edge whetted to the finest, untouched, keen, exquisite. I was young; I had good health; pleasure and I had never met. . . . Well! and what did I see? I will tell you faithfully. Green, reedy swamps; fields, fertile but flat, cultivated in patches that made them look like magnified kitchen-gardens; belts of cut trees, formal as pollard willows, skirting the horizon; narrow canals, gliding slow by the road-side; painted Flemish farmhouses; some very dirty hovels; a gray, dead sky; wet road, wet fields, wet house-tops: not a beautiful, scarcely a picturesque object met my eye along the whole route; yet to me, all was beautiful, all was more than picturesque. (201-02)

Yet behind Crimsworth's gentle irony against his younger self is a much tougher irony which the narrator fails to see. Brontë would have us note that in correcting the perceptions of his younger self, Crimsworth often encloses himself more tightly into a set of highly inadequate attitudes.

We see these ironies operating in Crimsworth's feelings about the students of Zoraïde Reuter's school. Noticing that the window in his room which opens onto the girls' garden is boarded up (an enclosure image of his young blindness), he feels a strong desire to see behind the boards. He imagines the ground in the garden to be "consecrated," a paradise where angels play. When he is finally hired to teach at the girls' school, he is delighted. "'I shall now at last see the mysterious garden: I shall gaze both on the angels and their Eden'" (216). All the humour of the delusion is enjoyed by Crimsworth the narrator. He describes his process of disillusionment with the girls:

> Daily, as I continued my attendance at the seminary of Mdlle. Reuter, did I find fresh occasions to compare the ideal with the real. What had I known of female character previously to my arrival at Brussels? Precious little. And what was my notion of it? Something vague, slight, gauzy, glittering; now when I came in contact with it I found it to be a palpable substance enough; very hard too sometimes, and often heavy; there was metal in it, both lead and iron. (231)

But the quasi-objective tone of Crimsworth's voice of experience immediately gives itself the lie. He offers to "open his portfolio" (231) to sketch a few students, and proceeds to reveal his barely suppressed disgust and rage at the girls. His three pictures "from the life" (234) are painted by a vengeful, moralistic hand. One girl he refers to as an "unnatural-looking being," "Gorgon-like," who practises "panther-like deceit" (232). He seems capable of only the crudest kind of adversary relationship with the girls (the way they look at him is their "artillery" [233]), and falls back on his over-simplified moral abstractions in order to place them within his scheme ("Mutiny" and "Hate" are graved on Juanna's brow [234]). When Crimsworth physically confines one of the girls (locks her up in a cabinet), he is only echoing the mental confinement that his descriptions reflect.

What his attitude toward the girls reveals, then, is the constriction of Crimsworth's ostensibly maturing perceptions. Crimsworth approaches his students with naïve idealism; when forced to adjust, he castigates the real rather than tempering the ideal. As we shall see, his ideal remains intact—pent, perhaps, in another strait and secret nook—waiting only for the appropriate woman to be forced into its contracted boundaries.

Before turning to a consideration of the other main characters in the book, it would be useful to note a final pair of images which corroborates the idea of Crimsworth's mental enclosure. As I have noted, the pictures Crimsworth frames of his world are idiosyncratic—a personalized way of imposing a rationale on a perplexing life. Crimsworth is aware of the differences between himself and other people. Early in the novel, he reveals his feelings of separateness to Hunsden with a certain smug satisfaction: "'I must follow my own devices—I must till the day of my death; because I can neither comprehend, adopt, nor work out those of other people'" (198). Crimsworth's image for himself in the novel's early chapters is as an Israelite in Egypt. Orphaned, confined to drudgery in the counting-house of his unsympathetic brother Edward, he characterizes his work as a "task thankless and bitter as that of the Israelite crawling over the sun-baked fields of Egypt in search of straw and stubble wherewith to accomplish his tale of bricks" (190). The image is apt in several ways. His work is futile; he lives in bondage. But most important, Crimsworth is elevating his separateness into the virtue of a martyr. As an Israelite, he is not only victim, but chosen one. A large part of his self-delusion pertains to a puritanical notion of himself as an anti-sensualist in a world of flesh-pots. Beginning with a reference to his wealthy cousins in the letter to Charles, Crimsworth sets himself apart from women whose attractions he considers himself above. Not for him are the base sexual yearnings of the normal man.[17] (The pronounced element of twisted sexuality in his accounts of his students is an ironic contradiction of his high-mindedness.) But his attitude toward women is only one important element in Crimsworth's Israelite conception of himself. The notion of his own special nature exists in Crimsworth's mind as a means by which to exempt himself, with self-congratulatory glibness, from the humbling exigencies of self-knowledge.

Set off against the Israelite in Crimsworth's mind is a parallel image in the reader's. Brontë very delicately introduces an association between Crimsworth and another literary figure, one not quite so sombre as the Israelite in Egypt. When Crimsworth refers, while observing the Belgian landscape, to a "Brobdignagian [sic] kitchen-garden" (282), we realize that he is not so unlike another fellow-traveller. Associated with Gulliver's innocence, sexual repression, fastidiousness, and, above all, pride, William Crimsworth becomes a figure considerably less elevated than the Israelite. Like Gulliver's, Crimsworth's innocence is not ennobling, but constricting—his pride not a source of dignity, but of self-aggrandizement. The two images coexist, then, as suggestively ironic pieces in the puzzle of Crimsworth's character. Lurking just on the surface is Brontë's suggestion that Crimsworth's idea of his separateness may transform him from his own sublime into the reader's ridiculous. Crimsworth leaves England—his Egypt—in search of the Canaan which he not only feels he deserves but also can use to vindicate his uniqueness. But the reader has discovered that the Israelite's bondage was considerably more than physical.

II.   Hunsden, Reuter, and Frances Henri:
Portrait and Pentimento

Although he enjoys portraying his life as a series of pictures, William Crimsworth remains oblivious to the pentimento which complicates his literary self-portraiture. The personal myth he constructs seems to the reader to be superimposed upon a life which is far less tidy than Crimsworth himself will acknowledge. Presented with the official Crimsworth, we remain constantly aware—though the outlines are never distinct—of the traces of a second image beneath. In the portraits of the other main characters in the novel—Hunsden, Zoraïde Reuter, and Frances Henri—the pentimento is equally pronounced, and equally indistinct. We are presented with their images as seen through the eyes of Crimsworth; yet the shadows of images that Crimsworth does not see flicker always before us.

Although Hunsden Yorke Hunsden is a friend of long standing (he is the only character besides Crimsworth to exist all the way through the novel), Crimsworth's attitude to him is always acrimonious. He presents Hunsden as a presumptuous, eccentric person—a person who seems not to know that he is meant to be of secondary importance in the Crimsworth autobiography. The man who seems irritatingly idiosyncratic to Crimsworth, however, strikes the reader as ironically appropriate. For, viewed in relation to Crimsworth, Hunsden is a running commentary on the protagonist's limitations. Like Crimsworth, he has both the tradesman and the aristocrat in his lineage—but unlike Crimsworth, he is at home in the world. Like Crimsworth, he is a mixture of masculine and feminine characteristics—but unlike Crimsworth, he has the confidence to address aggressively a challenging world. Where Crimsworth is fastidious and constricted, Hunsden is generous and expansive (though the misanthropic directness of Hunsden's speech seems to Crimsworth to be far less kindly than his own minced words). Like Crimsworth, Hunsden has a feminine ideal—but unlike Crimsworth, his ideal coexists with a strong strain of practicality. He can live enthusiastically with the ideal unfulfilled. And finally, like Crimsworth, Hunsden is unique—but whereas Crimsworth's uniqueness exists only in his mind, as a means of separating himself from a tawdry world, Hunsden's uniqueness is palpable. Perhaps that is why he defies even Crimsworth's self-confident descriptive powers: "There is no use in attempting to describe," says Crimsworth, "what is indescribable" (308). The close similarities—and awesome differences—between the two men explain why Crimsworth is so perpetually vulnerable to his friend.

Hunsden is responsible for almost all the good fortune in Crimsworth's career; but he can also be called Crimsworth's nemesis. For reasons which are not quite clear, his early interest in Crimsworth abides throughout the novel. He precipitates the release from Edward's tyranny, makes the crucial referral for a teaching job in Belgium, and buys the only one of Crimsworth's pictures which is ever really important—that of his mother—as an unsolicited gift. But Hunsden's generosity is always resented by Crimsworth. In an interesting juxtaposition of scenes, Brontë demonstrates the ease with which Crimsworth can accept favours from another benefactor, Victor Vandenhuten, as compared with the bitterness that Hunsden's help always elicits. From Crimsworth's description of Vandenhuten, we infer the cause: "in short our characters dovetailed, but my mind having more fire and action than his, instinctively assumed and kept the predominance" (317). With Hunsden, Crimsworth can never keep the predominance; something within him must realize that his friend represents the authentic product of which he is himself only an unconvincing reproduction. The ironic connections between the two men are never completely brought to the consciousness of Crimsworth the narrator—nor, as we shall see, is the implicit threat that Hunsden poses to the autobiographer's happy ending.

Crimsworth's first love, Zoraïde Reuter, is also a victim of his misanthropy. The process of disillusionment which Crimsworth underwent with his students is echoed with Reuter. And echoed as well are the aging Crimsworth's sage amusement at the naïveté of his younger self, and the reader's distance from both narrators. Even at her best, Reuter hardly resembles the Angels in their Eden; she taxes even Crimsworth's ability to idealize. Yet, with great effort, the young man manages to rationalize his love. At their first meeting, he is patronizingly amused by the business talent of a young woman. He must be growing wiser, he feels, since he can admire the "crafty little politician" (226). And if Reuter does not quite fit the "female character as depicted in Poetry and Fiction" (226), she is only a more interesting challenge. When pressed for a rationale by which to justify himself, young Crimsworth is ingenious enough to fall back on religious prejudice: "She has been brought up a Catholic: had she been born an Englishwoman, and reared a Protestant, might she not have added straight integrity to all her other excellences? Supposing she were to marry an English and Protestant husband, would she not, rational, sensible, as she is, quickly acknowledge the superiority of right over expediency, honesty over policy?" (240). The scene in which Crimsworth conveys his strongest moment of infatuation takes place in that touchstone of his romantic imagination, the garden of the Pensionnat:

In another minute I and the directress were walking side by side down the valley bordered with fruit-trees, whose white blossoms were then in full blow as well as their tender green leaves. The sky was blue, the air still, the May afternoon was full of brightness and fragrance. Released from the stifling class, surrounded with flowers and foliage, with a pleasing, smiling, affable woman at my side—how did I feel? Why, very enviably. It seemed as if the romantic visions my imagination had suggested of this garden, while it was yet hidden from me by the jealous boards, were more than realised; and, when a turn in the alley shut out the view of the house, and some tall shrubs excluded M. Pelet's mansion, and screened us momentarily from the other houses, rising amphitheatre-like round this green spot, I gave my arm to Mdlle. Reuter, and led her to a garden-chair, nestled under some lilacs near. She sat down; I took my place at her side. She went on talking to me with that ease which communicates ease, and, as I listened, a revelation dawned in my mind that I was on the brink of falling in love. (238)

Writing from Daisy Lane, Crimsworth contrives the scene of his young delusion neatly. In retrospect, he sees the garden as the perfect location for the growth of his younger, callow self from innocence to experience.[18] For the reader, however, the garden is yet another enclosure, reflecting ironically upon both the young lover and his wiser, older self. And the author's irony becomes more stringent when, after the inevitable disillusionment, young and old Crimsworth agree in their interpretation of the event.

Appropriately, the disillusionment takes place in the same garden. Crimsworth, dreaming of Reuter at his now unboarded window, hears voices below. It is Reuter and Pelet, talking of their wedding plans, and of him. Neither the old nor the young Crimsworth understands the inadequacy of his response to his disillusionment. The love arose solely from Crimsworth's romantic mind. Yet both Crimsworths view the overheard conversation as an act of treachery, strong enough to extinguish all "faith in love and friendship" (242). The shared vision of old and young Crimsworth is demonstrated through the mixing of past and present tenses:

Not that I nursed vengeance—no; but the sense of insult and treachery lived in me like a kindling, though as yet smothered coal. God knows I am not by nature vindictive; I would not hurt a man because I can no longer trust or like him; but neither my reason nor feelings are of the vacillating order—they are not of that sand-like sort where impressions, if soon made, are as soon effaced. Once convinced that my friend's disposition is incompatible with my own, once assured that he is indelibly stained with certain defects obnoxious to my principles, and I dissolve the connection. (242-43)

Also echoed here are the familiar tones of Crimsworth's moralism: his castigation of whatever fails to live up to his mind-forged ideals, and his claims to a special, exalted nature. As we would expect, he calls on an abstraction

—Reason—to be his physician after suffering the blow. Regardless of what his older self may think, Crimsworth has not learned much; his mind remains as sealed off as Mlle Reuter's "allée défendue."

Thenceforward, Crimsworth's bitterness and distrust regarding Zoraïde Reuter are extreme. Though Reuter continues to be crafty and manipulative, she apparently falls in love with Crimsworth and is treated very cruelly indeed. (The garden again becomes an emblem of Crimsworth's constricted perceptions.) By the time Reuter fires Frances Henri (probably with at least some justification), Crimsworth's disdain for the directress has turned into loathing. He has successfully reduced a complicated woman to the status of a bad angel.

In Crimsworth's mind, Reuter is an unattractive foil for his heart's desire, Frances. He sees Reuter as fully engaged in her world, Frances as an outsider; Reuter as manipulative, Frances as passive; Reuter as hardened, Frances as tender; Reuter as contrived, Frances as natural; Reuter as self-protective, Frances as vulnerable. Yet the novel suggests that as telling as the differences between the two women are their similarities. First, their careers are parallel: Frances, like Reuter, will become the directress of her own school. But more important, Reuter makes guarded suggestions of deeper similarities between them. "'Her present position,'" she says, "'has once been mine, or nearly so; it is then but natural I should sympathise with her...'" (254). Within this enigmatic comment, and also within the feelings of animosity between the two women, lurks the possibility, borne out by more direct evidence elsewhere, that Frances Henri is not what Crimsworth believes her to be.

Although critics have tended to see only Crimsworth's romanticized portrait of Frances, there is ample evidence in *The Professor* that Brontë's portrait, which lurks behind Crimsworth's, is meant to be considerably more subtle, complicated, and ambiguous. First, there are a number of hints that Frances may not always have lived the sheltered, virginal life which Crimsworth complacently assumes she has. Early in their acquaintance, Frances describes her life in Switzerland as being "'in a circle; I walked the same round every day'" (266). She speaks of knowing something of the "'bourgeois of Geneva'" and of Brussels (266). And echoing the suggestiveness of these remarks is Reuter's; the older woman says of Frances that she does "'not like her going out in all weathers'" (276). Later, Frances mentions the frustrations of "'people who are only in each other's company for amusement'" (328-29). And on several occasions she calmly entertains Crimsworth in her apartment alone.[19]

The evidence for Frances' questionable past is not obtrusive. Rather it is composed of delicately suggestive allusions which only hint at something Crimsworth cannot see. Whether or not she has had a sexual past, though, Frances certainly has had some kind of experience in her life that Crimsworth has not. Both her pronounced independence and her unmistakable emotional separateness from him do not correspond to Crimsworth's portrait of her. The very moment she accepts his proposal of marriage, for example, Frances asks to be allowed to continue teaching (327-28). This hard-headed practicality, as well as her tears on her wedding day (342), indicates that for Frances the choice to marry is far from simple. Although Hunsden may be able to live successfully on his own, Frances does not have the male option of a completely independent life; she must know that spending life alone would mean abandoning her career ambitions. It is clear, then, that Frances' view of the marriage has complications that Crimsworth does not dream of; it is likely that she accepts the marriage proposal as the most attractive of several very limited options open to her.

Frances' "Jane" poem indicates that her need for a "master"—the side of her which Crimsworth emphasizes—is a substantial part of her nature. But as Brontë skilfully demonstrates through suggestive details, the deluded Crimsworth never understands the intricacies of his wife's position. He places her on the conventional pedestal, a pedestal which fits nicely into the myth he is creating of his own "successful" life. Yet Frances knows much more of the world than does her "master." When Crimsworth says of her that "I knew how the more dangerous flame [of passion] burned safely under the eye of reason" (285), he speaks as a puritan; he has no notion of how clearly that eye of reason really sees.

Part of what makes Frances particularly suitable to Crimsworth's autobiographical designs is the fact that she is as homeless as he. Their mutual rootlessness enables Crimsworth to circumvent a certain kind of social definition; it is another means by which Crimsworth can define himself as a man outside—and above—the rest of the world. He delights in Frances' *devoir* about the emigrant and is sensitive to her expressed desire for her own Canaan. The Israelite image which he adopted in the early chapters is appropriately transformed. Crimsworth's Egypt (England) becomes Frances' Canaan, and by means of a letter from Hunsden, the entire notion is ironically reversed. Hunsden imagines Crimsworth as an Israelite in Belgium, not England: "'sitting like a black-haired, tawny-skinned, long-nosed Israelite by the flesh-pots of Egypt'" (302). The implication is that Crimsworth would be a displaced Israelite wherever he lived; for him, exile is a state of mind. In choosing Frances, Crimsworth can cling to his feelings of being unique, and therefore special. As he speaks of Hunsden's knowledge of him, this need is apparent: "nor could he, keen-sighted as he was, penetrate into my heart, search my brain, and read my peculiar sympathies and antipathies; he had not known me long enough, or well enough, to perceive how long my feelings would ebb under some influences, powerful over most minds; how high, how fast they would flow under other influences, that perhaps acted with the more intense force on me, because they acted on me alone" (312).

If Frances' homelessness is a convenience for Crimsworth, so too is her role as his student. Brontë's frequent use of the teacher-student relationship has prompted many critics to suggest a questionable equivalence between the art and the life. Thus Inga-Stina Ewbank has called the teaching situation "an image of the ideal relationship" for Brontë.[20] In *The Professor*, however, teacher-student relationships are far from ideal: they are based, for the most part, on tyranny. As I have mentioned, Crimsworth relates to his students as an adversary: through his descriptions of the girls in Reuter's school he reveals both his constricted sexual nature and his related need for power. The same kind of problem is a factor in his relationship with Frances. Her status as a social and educational inferior provides easy superiority for Crimsworth; it enables him, through his autobiographical myth, to enclose her emotions into an even smaller nook than his own. There are several scenes when Crimsworth, forcing Frances to speak English with the ostensible purpose of benefiting her language development, becomes almost sadistic in his treatment of her. (And one such scene is the proposal scene.) The kind of dominance over Frances that Crimsworth seems to need is ironically undercut both by the specifics of their relationship and by the echoes of earlier student relationships.

Frances Henri, then, is just what Crimsworth needs. She has—on the surface, at least—precisely those qualities which enable him to impose a gratifying rationale on his life story. She is socially inferior, educationally disadvantaged, and rootless; a difficult life has made her both tractable and desperate for security. But complications arise for Crimsworth. In order to create the picture of his life in the way which gratifies him most, he must do something very earnest, very real: he must take a wife. The shaky foundations of his psychosexual nature catch up with him only moments after he proposes to Frances. His attack of hypochondria is one of Brontë's most interesting ways of revealing the irony of his mental enclosure.

In reading *The Professor* as a straightforward success story, most critics have had difficulty accounting for Crimsworth's bout of hypochondria. Robert Martin, for example, finds it to be "without any apparent relevance," and objects to its coming at a time when "Crimsworth's psychic health has never been better."[21] And Inga-Stina Ewbank reverts to Brontë biography to justify the scene: "Powerful in itself, this passage has no justification in plot or character; there is nothing either before or after to suggest such nervous sensibilities in the very sensible hero. His breakdown here is introduced, it would seem, only to give an excuse for what is a welling-up from the suppressed ego of the author."[22] These critical discussions, however, leave out what seems to me to be Brontë's major effort in the novel. Crimsworth is telling his own story, or, rather, presenting his own myth. While ostensibly creating art which will reflect his life, he is in reality moulding the life to fit the art. But, as Roy Pascal has observed about autobiography, "Consistent misrepresentation of oneself is not easy."[23] Like the other loose ends which Brontë insinuates before us, Crimsworth's attack of hypochondria qualifies his personal mythology. It represents, in Pascal's terms, a "gap" in his self-portrait, or, in James' terms, a "leakage" in his ostensibly watertight scheme. The attack of hypochondria may seem inconsistent to Crimsworth, but for the reader it is part of the pentimento.

Crimsworth's myth about himself, as I have mentioned, is based largely on his feelings of being different from others. An essential part of this difference is his view of himself as an anti-sensualist (a view which the reader has always discredited on the basis of his descriptions of his students). But just after proposing to Frances, he discovers that he is in fact strongly attracted physically to her. As he confesses to the reader: "It appeared then, that I too was a sensualist in my temperate and fastidious way" (329). Crimsworth's acceptance of his own sexual nature is followed immediately by the attack of hypochondria. Apparently his righteous self-delusions do not die easily. It is appropriate that the attack is described as claustrophobic, and as sexual. Crimsworth is imprisoned by hypochondria, who has the bony arms of a death-cold concubine:

> She had been my acquaintance, nay, my guest, once before in boyhood; I had entertained her at bed and board for a year; for that space of time I had her to myself in secret; she lay with me, she ate with me, she walked out with me, showing me nooks in woods, hollows in hills where we could sit together, and where she could drop her drear veil over me, and so hide sky and sun, grass and green tree; taking me entirely to her death-cold bosom, and holding me with arms of bone. . . .
> I repulsed her as one would a dreaded and ghastly concubine coming to embitter a husband's heart towards his young bride; in vain; she kept her sway over me for that night and the next day, and eight succeeding days. (330-31)

Crimsworth's amazement that the attack should come at this point in his life—"why did hypochondria accost me now?" (331)—is not shared by the reader. Having abandoned the safety of his clearly-defined self-image, he is bound to suffer greatly. Marriage to Frances (who is surely represented in part by the concubine) will of necessity involve psychic and physical realities which he has never before had to face.

If Crimsworth's pre-marital forebodings are complex, those of his new bride are even more so. During the early descriptions of their relationship, as I have noted, the reader continually senses that Crimsworth is not telling the entire story about Frances. Frances' behaviour strengthens this doubt. Perhaps the height of the reader's wonder about her comes in the remarkable scene when she meets Hunsden. Crimsworth takes a seat on the periphery of the room, thus characteristically removing himself and framing the participants in the spectacle. As he watches in supercilious amusement, his deferential, resigned, often vapid Frances suddenly becomes, as she converses with Hunsden, vital, daring, even sexual.

> Animated by degrees, she began to change, just as a grave night-sky changes at the approach of sunrise: first it seemed as if her forehead cleared, then her eyes glittered, her features relaxed, and became quite mobile; her subdued complexion grew warm and transparent; to me, she now looked pretty; before, she had only looked ladylike.
> She had many things to say to the Englishman just fresh from his island-country, and she urged him with an enthusiasm of curiosity, which ere long thawed Hunsden's reserve as fire thaws a congealed viper. I use this not very flattering comparison because he vividly reminded me of a snake waking from torpor, as he erected his tall form, reared his head, before a little declined, and putting back his hair from his broad Saxon forehead, showed unshaded the gleam of almost savage satire which his interlocutor's tone of eagerness and look of ardour had suffered at once to kindle in his soul and elicit from his eyes: he was himself, as Frances was herself, and in none but his own language would he now address her. (335)

Strangely, Frances' metamorphosis into a person of warmth, relaxation, and beauty does not threaten the complacent Crimsworth. Neither does the vitality of Hunsden who, imaged as a snake who is tempted by Frances, both ironically undercuts the couple's allegedly invulnerable love and also foreshadows their peculiar future. The scene closes with two literary references, both of which serve a purpose similar to that of the passage above. First, a reference to *Othello* reinforces the delicate suggestions of a love (between Frances and Crimsworth) built on a shaky foundation. And second, Hunsden's Byronic farewell, and Frances' positive response to it, emphasize again

37

the potential she has for stepping outside the rigid frame in which Crimsworth has enclosed her.

Throughout the Crimsworths' married life, Brontë continues her intimations that Frances' feelings differ from her husband's. What Crimsworth describes is his pleasure at Frances' continual deference to him, his pride in his own generosity (in allowing Frances to open her school), and his delight at playfully subduing her spirit when he "frequently dosed her with Wordsworth" (348). But though Frances' surface reactions may be just as Crimsworth sees them, they indicate, by now, a great deal more to the reader than they do to Crimsworth. Perhaps the clearest signals Brontë sends to the reader in the novel's final chapters come through the passages about young Victor. When Frances leaves Crimsworth's side to visit her sleeping baby, she "abandons" him. When Victor's dog Yorke is exposed to rabies, Crimsworth coldly shoots it, leaves the body for his young son to find, and then describes the entire scene with sanctimonious relish. As he turns away from Victor's grief, it is Frances who comforts their distraught child. And finally, when Crimsworth discusses his son's treatment at the hands of his gentle mother, we feel the full force of his puritanical rage:

> though Frances will not make a milksop of her son, she will accustom him to a style of treatment, a forbearance, a congenial tenderness, he will meet with from none else. She sees, as I also see, a something in Victor's temper —a kind of electrical ardour and power—which emits, now and then, ominous sparks; Hunsden calls it his spirit, and says it should not be curbed. I call it the leaven of the offending Adam, and consider that it should be, if not *whipped* out of him, at least soundly disciplined; and that he will be cheap of any amount of either bodily or mental suffering which will ground him radically in the art of self-control. . . . for that cloud on his bony brow—for that compression of his statuesque lips, the lad will some day get blows instead of blandishments—kicks instead of kisses; then for the fit of mute fury which will sicken his body and madden his soul; then for the ordeal of merited and salutary suffering, out of which he will come (I trust) a wiser and a better man. (357-58)

Crimsworth contemplates his son's suffering with chilling complacency. Frances, though she hides it from her husband, clearly has an independent relationship with—and independent opinions on—the boy. Frances seems, then, to have the same wider vision at the end of the novel that she has had throughout. She evidently goes through the motions of living up to Crimsworth's happy ending—but were she to tell the story, we feel certain that her version would be vastly different.

If the relations of the three Crimsworths to each other are ambiguous at the end of the novel, the relations of all of them to Yorke Hunsden are even more so. Hunsden is a strange presence in the Crimsworth family; Hunsden Wood, with its "winding ways," would seem to be a suggestive image of the tangled relations that may exist there. At several points, for instance, Crimsworth refers to the mutual affection between his son and Hunsden. Toward the end of the novel, he observes the two together:

> I see him now; he stands by Hunsden, who is seated on the lawn under the beech; Hunsden's hand rests on the boy's collar, and he is instilling God knows what principles into his ear.... Victor has a preference for Hunsden, full as strong as I deem desirable, being considerably more potent, decided, and indiscriminating, than any I ever entertained for that personage myself. (358)

As Crimsworth looks on at his son and Hunsden, apparently not deeply threatened when he witnesses their strong bond, we are reminded of the earlier scene in which he observed Hunsden and Frances with a similar complacency as they engaged in animated, almost sexually provocative, conversation. Earlier, Hunsden played the role of lover to Frances; in this scene, he would seem to be acting, at least metaphorically, as father to Victor. Indeed, the reader—accustomed by now to the alternative possibilities which lurk beneath Crimsworth's narrative—might even wonder whether the father-son relationship between Hunsden and Victor is only metaphorical. Perhaps, unbeknownst to Crimsworth, there is another family tree in Hunsden Wood in addition to his own. But whatever the actual relationships among Victor, Frances, and Hunsden may be—and no doubt we are not meant to be certain —Hunsden continues to be a dominant presence for all three members of the Crimsworth family. And, characteristically, Crimsworth continues to be oblivious to the complexities that surround him.

The moral universe of *The Professor* is decidedly postlapsarian. Crimsworth is the innocent of the novel; all the other characters are at home in a world of compromised ideals and limited expectations. Yet—realist that she was— Brontë does not castigate her characters for being less than perfect. It is Crimsworth's brand of innocence, which refuses to recognize the mixed state of humankind and retreats into complacency, that receives the sharpest blows. Only gradually does the reader realize that the novel's moral landscape borrows much of its dark tone from the short-sighted eyes through which it is perceived.

III.   The Fourth Picture: A "Golden Halo of Fiction"

In the novel's final moments, Crimsworth stops framing pictures; instead, he paints one. Although he makes no explicit reference to the fourth picture in the gallery of his life, the final pages in fact represent its unveiling. Crimsworth's fourth picture completes his presentation of his autobiographical myth. He construes an image of his life at Daisy Lane as his final Eden—the family living in an unsullied region, in a "picturesque and not too spacious dwelling" (351), surrounded by roses and ivy. Having discovered, as he thinks, the pitfalls of artificial gardens [24] and the snares of false delusions, he can now envisage his married life as the real paradise. In evoking his ostensible paradise, however, Crimsworth intensifies the dehumanizing natural images he has used throughout the novel's latter sections of his wife and son; they become birds, plants which he tends, or fruit. He had earlier enjoyed characterizing Frances to Hunsden as "an unique fruit, growing wild," tantalizingly natural in contrast to his friend's "hot-house grapes" (313). Now, having transplanted Frances into a rural setting, he revels in the appropriateness of the pastoral life he has created for his "dove," his "butterfly," his "precious plant."

Brontë's ironic manipulation of prelapsarian imagery did not begin with *The Professor*. In one of the earlier novelettes (*Caroline Vernon*, 1839), her unhappy heroine is banished to Eden-Cottage, near Fidena. For Caroline, the cottage becomes a prison; she flees from Eden into the unscrupulous arms of Zamorna.[25] Though not so extreme a torture, Daisy Lane must be for Frances considerably less Edenic than it is for her husband.

The love between Frances and Crimsworth began with the teacher finding his lost student mourning her aunt's death in a cemetery. Leading her from the graveyard, Crimsworth saw himself as effecting a rebirth—a victory over the forces of poverty, death, and an antagonistic world. But after rescuing Frances from the walled-in cemetery, Crimsworth merely substitutes one enclosure—his doubtful Paradise—for another. The thought of Frances and her lifelong partner is unsettling; Brontë might have been describing a Crimsworth when she wrote to Ellen Nussey that "a man with a weak brain, chill affections and a strong will—is merely an intractable fiend—you can have no hold of him—you can never lead him right."[26] With a husband, then, whose illusions require great tact to maintain, a son whose equilibrium is constantly threatened, and the emphatic figure of the serpent-like Hunsden lurking about the "winding ways" of the forest, Frances must find life at Daisy Lane considerably less than spacious.

Such is not the case for Crimsworth. The final enclosure he creates—the pastoral life at Daisy Lane—fulfills his need for an autobiographical rationale as satisfactorily as have all his other techniques for containing experience. Virtually every critic who has written on *The Professor* has commented on Crimsworth's growth during the course of the novel.[27] Yet Crimsworth has not changed essentially since the letter to Charles; only his situation is different. The ironic thrust of Crimsworth's success story is based upon the tension between worldly success and personal delusion. Crimsworth's need to superimpose his mental enclosures onto the world around him has resulted in appalling insensitivity. In the world of *The Professor*, innocence can be considerably darker than experience.

Midway through the novel, in a passage often used to characterize *The Professor*, Crimsworth states his opinion on the kinds of pictures novelists should paint:

> Novelists should never allow themselves to weary of the study of real life. If they observed this duty conscientiously, they would give us fewer pictures chequered with vivid contrasts of light and shade.... (277)

Brontë's success in giving us real life is achieved by means of Crimsworth's failure; in spite of himself, he manages nothing but a "golden halo of fiction" (299). As he ends his story, art appropriately catches up to life, and in fact overtakes it. Crimsworth writes his last page at the moment he lives it; the presence by his side of Frances, who is waiting tea for him, is as pleasant, he says, "as the perfume of the fresh hay and spicy flowers, as the glow of the westering sun, as the repose of the midsummer eve are to my senses" (359). We are not surprised to find Crimsworth so much more engaged in the appearance on his page than in the reality at his elbow. At the penultimate moment, as throughout the tale, art is more real to him than life. "But Hunsden comes." As this familiar intruder forces his presence into the room which frames the family ("disturbing," as Crimsworth writes, "two bees and a butterfly"), we note once again the instability of the autobiographer's smug portrait of blissful domesticity. Crimsworth's hackneyed ending, like all his autobiographical efforts, defeats its own purpose.

CHAPTER THREE

Jane Eyre

The "chill of despair"[1] which invaded Currer Bell's heart as *The Professor* met with one rejection after another seems not to have delayed Brontë's second effort. When W. S. Williams of Smith, Elder and Co. sent, along with a sixth rejection, an expression of interest in subsequent novels, Brontë replied that *Jane Eyre* was already well under way.[2] Years later she mocked the taste for the romantic which had led publishers to refuse her first novel:

> ... I find that publishers in general ... would have liked something more imaginative and poetical—something more consonant with a highly wrought fancy, with a taste for pathos, with sentiments more tender, elevated, unworldly. Indeed, until an author has tried to dispose of a manuscript of this kind, he can never know what stores of romance and sensibility lie hidden in breasts he would not have suspected of casketing such treasures. Men in business are usually thought to prefer the real; on trial the idea will be often found fallacious: a passionate preference for the wild, wonderful, and thrilling—the strange, startling, and harrowing—agitates divers souls that show a calm and sober surface.[3]

In light of these remarks, it might at first seem strange that Brontë's second novel has an abundance of what publishers felt *The Professor* lacked: "the wild, wonderful, and thrilling." With a madwoman locked in an attic, well-timed visitations of lightning and fire, and a mystical call in the night from a distant lover, *Jane Eyre* seems on the surface to be a radical departure from the quietly ironic mode of *The Professor*.

Yet the differences between Brontë's first two novels are more apparent than real. To assume that in *Jane Eyre* Brontë turned to an entirely different kind of fiction is to miss the point of the novel. The popular view of *Jane Eyre* as "one of the finest achievements of the romantic sensibility"[4] raises many difficulties. Most important, this view confuses Jane's sensibility with that of her creator. Most readers have neglected the fact that *Jane Eyre*, as the title page of its first edition indicates, is a fictional autobiography. They have forgotten, as they did with *The Professor*, whose story the novel is meant to tell.[5]

Evidence that Jane Eyre must not be confused with Charlotte Brontë comes from many sources, among them Brontë's close associates. Harriet

Martineau explained in her obituary of Brontë that "Jane Eyre was naturally and universally supposed to be Charlotte herself; but she always denied it, calmly, cheerfully, and with the obvious sincerity which characterized all she said."[6] And George Smith, in his *Memoirs*, described the painful consequences suffered by Thackeray after he had, with great insensitivity, introduced Brontë to his mother as "Jane Eyre."[7]

But more intrinsic evidence for the distance between Brontë and her narrator is available. In the act of writing her novel, Brontë was especially careful to separate herself from Jane. The title page of the first edition cited Currer Bell as the editor, not author, of the tale told by Jane Eyre. Brontë herself, then, was even more removed from this story than from her first one. Jane Eyre narrated, Bell edited, and Brontë remained by choice in the distant background—the invisible begetter of the novel. Given the great amount of care Brontë took to back away from her storyteller, critics should beware of the tendency to take Jane's judgments as direct reflections of the author's.

Brontë, then, is not Jane Eyre, just as she was not William Crimsworth. And nowhere is the difference between author and autobiographer more apparent than in Jane's vulnerability to the excesses of her own imagination. Throughout the novel Jane's active artistic imagination shapes the image she presents of herself; clearly Brontë does not intend the reader to accept Jane's autobiographical image uncritically. Instead, she deliberately explores the limitations of romantic self-portraiture by using Jane as its skilful practitioner. It is a sad irony indeed that Brontë's strategy seems to have worked only too well; most readers, in her time and ours, have been so taken by the romantic surface of the novel that they have failed to recognize the author's deeper intention. Brontë's second novel has been misunderstood because it audaciously uses the materials it questions.

At least as much as *The Professor, Jane Eyre* was written to the dictates of the Brontë muse: the muse of the "severe Truth." But the autobiographers of the two novels deviate from this truth in strikingly different ways. In place of William Crimsworth's autobiographical mode, we are confronted with Jane Eyre's; rigid moralizing gives way to romantic imagining. William Crimsworth, as we have noted, enters his story smugly equipped with his personal mythology. We are never tempted, with Crimsworth, to identify with his feelings or to share his view of things. As we ponder his tightly constricted self-image, it gradually dissolves against the wider backdrop which Brontë provides. We remain—by his choice and our own—securely outside his strait and secret nook. Jane Eyre, on the other hand, has less pronounced boundaries around herself. She is a protean person, a person whose perspective fluctuates as she relates her life to us. Lawrence Jay Dessner emphasizes Jane's narrative complexity when he refers to "a continuum of Jane Eyres":

> At various stages of the story, young Jane acts and also comments and reports on her earlier actions and thoughts, and all of this is presented in turn by the mature Jane who is herself in a continuous state of action and change. For the mature Jane, in the process of reporting her story, reads herself back into it, forgets her present state, and relives her past, in ever-varying degrees. But she also judges her past, at times severely. Thus she creates in herself a continuum of attitudes, shifting between the poles of sympathetic identification with her young self and objective judgment of her past errors.[8]

Considering Jane's changing perspective, it is not surprising that, as Brontë herself once noted, the novel "produces a very different effect on different natures."[9]

Jane is also more attractive and expansive than Crimsworth; often she solicits and earns her reader's ungrudging assent. Unlike Crimsworth, Jane is not someone whom we wish either to dismiss entirely or to place outside the boundaries of our own natures. Encountering her first as an oppressed ten-year-old child, we are drawn to her by our own participation in the genesis and unfolding of her personality. Crimsworth, we recall, relates his story as a fully-formed—even fossilized—autobiographer; Jane forthrightly takes the reader along with her to experience the process of her life. Considering the many points at which Jane gains our sympathy, it is tempting to assume that when the narrator speaks, so does the author. But although Jane's autobiographical quest is deeply engaging, we must in the end take exception—as her creator does—to her "preference for the wild, wonderful, and thrilling."

I. The Unlocked Room

When we first meet her, Jane Eyre is in an enclosure. Banished from the company of the Reeds, the ten-year-old child seeks solace in a curtained window seat. But though she is "shrined in double retirement,"[10] Jane is considerably less secure in her enclosure than was William Crimsworth in his casque with the visor down. Only clear panes of glass protect her from the "drear November day" (4); and as John Reed soon demonstrates, she is extremely vulnerable to intruders.

If Crimsworth's secure enclosures implied his rigid mental constrictions—his well-defined personal mythologies—Jane's unprotected hideaway suggests the opposite. As her ambivalent attitudes in the early chapters suggest, Jane, both as character and as autobiographer, lacks Crimsworth's secure sense of self. As the novel begins, for example, she implies disappointment that there was "no possibility of taking a walk that day" (3); but then she immediately decides that she dislikes walks anyway. And later she reveals a more substantial inner conflict after her outburst at Mrs. Reed:

A ridge of lighted heath, alive, glancing, devouring, would have been a meet emblem of my mind when I accused and menaced Mrs. Reed: the same ridge, black and blasted after the flames are dead, would have represented as meetly my subsequent condition, when half an hour's silence and reflection had shewn me the madness of my conduct, and the dreariness of my hated and hating position.
Something of vengeance I had tasted for the first time; as aromatic wine it seemed on swallowing, warm and racy: its after-flavour, metallic and corroding, gave me a sensation as if I had been poisoned. (40-41)

Unable to condone her own emotional triumph, Jane herself supplies the reproach that Mrs. Reed would have administered.

Jane's conflicting emotional impulses as a child are echoed by the conflicting perceptions of her older self. Throughout the Gateshead chapters Jane the autobiographer presents opposing views of herself as a child, views to which she seems equally committed. On the one hand she portrays a pathetic orphan who is persecuted by the arbitrary whims of the callous Reeds; yet even as she evokes this image of herself, she undercuts it:

I was a discord in Gateshead-hall: I was like nobody there: I had nothing in harmony with Mrs. Reed or her children, or her chosen vassalage. If they did not love me, in fact, as little did I love them. They were not bound to regard with affection a thing that could not sympathize with one amongst them; a heterogeneous thing, opposed to them in temperament, in capacity, in propensities; a useless thing, incapable of serving their interest, or adding to their pleasure; a noxious thing, cherishing the germs of indignation at their treatment, of contempt of their judgment. (13-14)

Jane's poignant presentation of herself as a "rebel slave" (19) has behind it much warmth and energy. But at the same time, she frequently empathizes with the Reeds, and casts a cold eye on that "noxious thing," her passionate, childish self. Referring to Mrs. Reed's callous attitude toward her in the Red Room, Jane explains that "I was a precocious actress in her eyes" (16). But immediately afterward, she implies assent to that very attitude when she notes that "unconsciousness closed the scene." In *The Professor*, we sensed, Brontë was behind the scenes, qualifying Crimsworth's views of himself; in this story, the autobiographer often makes her own qualifications.

Throughout her autobiography Jane continues, at least as often as Crimsworth did, to enclose herself. But all of Jane's enclosures, unlike Crimsworth's, are as insecure as her window-seat.[11] What she seeks from that early enclosure is sanctuary from the "severe Truth"[12] of life with the Reeds; she hopes to make things clearer by turning away from her conflicts. But Jane's life—both inner and outer—never becomes tidy; her choices are never made without ambivalence. Whether prompted by the difficulties of her relations with the Reeds, by her conflicting desires about marriage to Rochester, or by her simultaneous fascination and repulsion for St. John Rivers, Jane's many attempts to enclose herself represent her many attempts to find a clear self-definition. Her rooms, her houses, her window-seat all signify that she is uncomfortable with unassimilated impulses, that she needs certainties in the midst of an uncertain life.

If Crimsworth sought in his autobiography to defend his complacent personal myth, Jane Eyre is seeking in hers to develop such a myth. She is an artist who has not yet arrived at a clear notion of herself; her autobiography embodies the search. Yet unhappily for Jane, the rooms in which she seeks security remain unlocked. In every instance of the nocturnal wanderings of Bertha the Thornfield nemesis, for example, Jane—by forgetting bolt or curtain—leaves herself open to intrusion. Jane's enclosures, throughout her story, will not seal her off from the complexities that threaten her. Faced with the contradictions of her life, she will find simple clarity unattainable.

To note that Jane seeks in her window-seat a refuge from the Reeds is to tell only part of the story. For if Jane, in her first enclosure, is turning away from something, she is also turning toward something. She has as her companion in the window-seat a book "stored with pictures" (4), pictures which feed her imagination just as Bessie's "passages of love and adventure taken from old fairy tales and older ballads" (5) do. The pictures are heightened correlatives of Jane's own situation; in them she sees her sad existence writ large. Thus the "drear November day" (4) of Jane's world is echoed in a major key by the bleak shores of the Arctic Zone; Jane's feeling of loneliness with the Reeds is answered in Bewick by a desolate coast and a solitary churchyard. Enclosed with her book, Jane fears "nothing but interruption" (5). As she flees the complexities of the world, she embraces the solace of her imagination. If Crimsworth found his peace in easy moral patterns, Jane seeks hers in art. But we note with a sense of foreboding that almost immediately (in the hands of John Reed), Jane's book of pictures becomes the instrument of her injury. From the beginning, Jane's "passionate preference for the wild, wonderful, and thrilling" is an uncertain refuge.

II. An Irregular Autobiography

In *The Professor*, the imagery of aesthetics heightens, but does not transform, the autobiographical material. The pictures that Crimsworth frames serve his purpose of sealing himself off from the world, and Brontë's purpose of ironically revealing this self-protectiveness to the reader. They do not, however, change the nature of the tale. In *Jane Eyre*, art is a more central concern; to a much greater extent than her predecessor, this autobiographer is a practising artist. William Crimsworth chronicles the events on his road to success, but Jane Eyre creates a work of art. In her second treatment of the form, Brontë created an artist who pushed autobiography a great distance in the direction of the novel.

Jane takes far greater liberties than Crimsworth in shaping her life. Crimsworth's omissions of some events and emphases on others advance his personal interpretations, but Jane, in shaping her life, virtually transforms it into a five-act play. She violates the probabilities of time, place, and person; the chronology of a life is devastated as she reduces ten years to a matter of months and skips entirely an eight-year period. And further contrivance is imparted by Jane's well-known pairings of characters: the Reeds and the Rivers, St. John and Rochester. When she explains to us that "this is not to be a regular autobiography" (98), we are struck by her understatement. Jane dissolves the boundaries between history and fiction, between autobiography and the novel. As her story progresses, we feel increasingly uncertain about what is life and what is art.

The overlapping boundaries of life and art are apparent in the many pictures which figure in the novel. Some useful critical attention has been devoted in recent years to the genesis and meaning of Jane's pictures.[18] What has not been discussed, however, is the larger issue of the relation between Jane the painter and Jane the autobiographer. If the pictures reveal aspects of Jane's character, they also reveal the contours of the endeavour in which she is engaged: creating her life story.

Unlike the paintings in William Crimsworth's gallery, Jane Eyre's pictures are rarely still-lifes. And her repertoire has an impressive range—all the way from phantasmagoria to quiet heads in charcoal. But Jane's pictures have a peculiar inability to stay in frames. All of the styles of the pictures are echoed again and again by similar verbal images and situations throughout the story. So often do scenes echo paintings that we begin to suspect we are dealing with canvas rather than printed page. Thus, after a happy day at Lowood, Jane draws ideal pictures in her mind—pictures which evoke pastoral repose:

... I feasted instead on the spectacle of ideal drawings, which I saw in
the dark; all the work of my own hands; freely pencilled houses and
trees, picturesque rocks and ruins, Cuyp-like groups of cattle, sweet paintings of butterflies hovering over unblown roses, of birds pecking at ripe
cherries, of wrens' nests enclosing pearl-like eggs, wreathed about with
young ivy sprays. (87)

The similar tone of the scene Jane describes just prior to meeting Rochester
reminds us of her affinity for ideal drawings:

If a breath of air stirred, it made no sound here; for there was not a
holly, not an evergreen to rustle, and the stripped hawthorn and hazel
bushes were as still as the white, worn stones which causewayed the middle of the path. Far and wide, on each side, there were only fields, where
no cattle now browsed; and the little brown birds which stirred occasionally in the hedge, looked like single russet leaves that had forgotten to
drop. (134)

And of course the well-known Edenic proposal scene has similar associations:
life and art have dissolved into each other.

Parallel in function to Jane's ideal drawings are the turbulent, Romantic
paintings of her young imagination—paintings of polar winters, streaming
hair, eerie moonlight. These paintings, of course, have an even fuller history
than the pastoral scenes. They come (somewhat transformed) from the pages
of Bewick; and they merge, as their frames melt away, into Bertha and
the ghostly third floor.

Finally, there are Jane's portraits: Rochester, Blanche Ingram, Rosamond
Oliver, and Jane herself. These pictures too connect the visual artist with
the word-painter. For we never get a fixed image of the people in these
drawings. Jane creates the portraits to contain and control feelings (her own
and others') rather than to represent her subjects. As her imagination advances and retreats, creates and refines, we are forced to see characters, as
well as their visual images, as somehow arbitrary, as made things. The inter-
relation between visual and verbal presentation dissolves the boundary between what is inside Jane's frames and what is outside. Both partake of the
same substance; both emphasize the invented quality of the entire work.
When Jane, at the end of her autobiography, assumes the role of word-
painter for the blind Rochester and shapes the entire image of his world,
she is only devoting more time to an already well-practised skill.

For Jane Eyre, then, the distinctions between art and life are never quite
clear. Her ostensible transcript of experience is in fact a work of art. We
read it as something that hovers precariously in a strange land—a land

halfway between what happened in the outer world of Jane's experience and in the inner world of her imagination. If Jane muddies the distinctions, however, we do not feel that she is deliberately attempting to dupe us (as, for example, Lucy Snowe—Brontë's consummate artist—does in *Villette*). In fact, Jane is if anything a rather ingenuous autobiographer; she tells things basically as she has perceived them. It is the nature of her perceptions, however, that creates difficulties for us—and, more importantly, difficulties for Jane. For, with her artist's eye, she is always in danger of transforming the concrete into the symbolic, the ordinary into the mythic. She is always in danger of living her life, and of telling it, by colouring her world of actual experience with the larger-than-life world of aesthetic experience.

An example of this colouring occurs when Jane decides to leave Lowood after the departure of Miss Temple. Unsettled by her characteristically conflicting impulses, she paces the floor of her room. She feels the need for change and stimulation, but is skeptical about her own tendency to harbour unrealistic hopes. When finally she thinks of the phrase "a new servitude" (102), she finds it excitingly appropriate. She looks upon it as a gratifying compromise between her dreams and her skepticism about these dreams.[14] Yet in arriving at her formula—for a formula it certainly is—Jane does not recognize her own need to elevate even domestic employment into something of romance. "A new servitude" is hardly a phrase that describes the normal existence of most maids and governesses: only Cinderella would find life so intense. What Jane's formula fails to allow for is the tedious, everyday existence that is neither painful sacrifice nor exciting fulfillment. As she casts around in her autobiography for formulas by which to contain her experience, she often grasps for just this kind of heightened intensity. In the world of art, such formulas pertain, but real life, as the novel will demonstrate, is not so thrilling.

Jane is never more vulnerable to the power of her imagination than when she paces the third floor at Thornfield Hall. Early in the novel she describes the gratifications of that dreamy, elevated sanctuary:

> my sole relief was to walk along the corridor of the third story, backwards and forwards, safe in the silence and solitude of the spot, and allow my mind's eye to dwell on whatever bright visions rose before it—and certainly they were many and glowing; to let my heart be heaved by the exultant movement which, while it swelled it in trouble, expanded it with life; and, best of all, to open my inward ear to a tale that was never ended—a tale my imagination created, and narrated continuously; quickened with all of incident, life, fire, feeling, that I desired and had not in my actual existence. (132)

The "bright visions" that Jane finds within her own imagination are comforting to her in the same way that the pictures from Bewick and Bessie's fairy tales were: they calm her unsettled nature. But more specifically, as these remarks indicate, the imagination offers Jane, again and again, "a tale that was never ended—a tale my imagination created, and narrated continuously." The visions of the imagination—of daydreams, fairy tales, and unworldly fiction—can go on forever. (We recall that in her window-seat, Jane feared "nothing but interruption.") And the tedium of everyday life need not intervene. Dominated by her romantic imagination, Jane clings to the hope of living both intensely and happily ever after. If her imagination offers her clarity, it is a clarity which makes unrealistic promises: it will never descend to the quotidian, and it will never end. The myth that Jane seeks for herself in her irregular autobiography, as her eventual "happy ending" will reveal, cannot abide.

III. "To Magnify Their Persons": [15]
Jane Eyre and Her World

If Jane Eyre differs from William Crimsworth as both person and artist, she also addresses a very different kind of world. Crimsworth, as we noted, darkens the landscape of his autobiography through his sombre perceptions of what is outside himself. But Jane, to a certain extent, rebuilds the landscape of her experience. Brontë's second autobiographer does not, like Crimsworth, remain oblivious to the truth of her life; rather, she attempts, through her art, to transform that truth into something of special value.

The people in Jane Eyre's world, like the episodes in her life, partake of the artifice of aesthetic creation. Under Jane's shaping hand, they move in the direction of the mythic. The strokes by which Jane paints her people are bold, the contrasts between them stark. Brocklehurst the black pillar is set off against Rivers the white marble statue; the ascetic Eliza contrasts with the self-indulgent Georgiana. The representative significance of Jane's associates often seems more important to her than their individual character. Rather than the specificity of a Zoraïde Reuter we encounter the intensity of a Blanche Ingram. A critic has written that the characters at the house party reveal "Jane's high degree of distorting involvement";[16] taken as a more general description of Jane's artistic technique, the phrase could apply to the entire world outside the boundaries of her own person.

Yet to say that we can recognize Jane's hand in the characters she creates is not to say that we should disregard their separate existence. The relation between subject and object is an ambiguous one in the novel, but one that we nevertheless must accept. Jane's characters are at the same time both inside herself and outside herself. If they seem partly to be figments of her creative imagination, they are also separate beings who elicit pronounced reactions from her.

The characters in Jane's life are of crucial importance in her search for a personal mythology. Her means of defining herself differs considerably from that of William Crimsworth and Lucy Snowe. The other two autobiographers have created their own definitions before they begin their stories; Jane, however, attempts to develop hers by responding to the myths of the people she meets. For the most part these people possess the certainty that Jane lacks. Smugly self-satisfied, they address Jane as a potential convert to their scheme of things.

Jane's first significant encounter with complacency comes when she meets Mr. Brocklehurst. Her vivid imagination transforms him within seconds from a black marble clergyman to a fairy-tale villain:

> What a face he had, now that it was almost on a level with mine! what a great nose! and what a mouth! and what large prominent teeth! (33-34)

She can perceive him only as larger than life; like Red Riding Hood's wolf, he evokes a pure childish terror.[17] Later, at Lowood, Brocklehurst is equally threatening to Jane. Her notion of him as a vengeful deity is deflated by the common sense of Helen Burns: "'Mr. Brocklehurst is not a god; nor is he even a great and admired man'" (10).

Jane is unable to establish any distance on Mr. Brocklehurst because his monolithic system of values threatens her unsettled (and therefore vulnerable) nature. With absolute certainty Brocklehurst makes a distinction between nature and grace:

> "Julia's hair curls naturally," returned Miss Temple, still more quietly.
> "Naturally! Yes but we are not to conform to nature: I wish these girls to be the children of Grace...." (73)

Brocklehurst, with complete conviction, advocates the repudiation of what is human for the sake of what he takes to be divine. From the time of her childhood at Gateshead, Jane has been unable to reconcile the claims of her natural, passional, impulses with the equally strong claims of self-renouncing submission to her lot.[18] Brocklehurst's neat split between heavenly and earthly speaks to her confusion. She is repelled, but fascinated, by the simplicity of his system.

Jane's extreme horror of Mr. Brocklehurst is equalled by her extreme adulation of Helen Burns. If Brocklehurst attracts by his tyranny, Helen

51

attracts by her submissiveness; both evoke the extremes of Jane's unsettled soul. Throughout their friendship, Jane remains incredulous about Helen's complete independence from other human beings; she interrogates Helen insistently about her firm preference for the afterlife. Yet ultimately she finds —or tries to find—in Helen the religious ideal for which Mr. Brocklehurst is the foil. She fails to see that Helen's solution is not at all unlike Brocklehurst's: it totally separates nature from grace. In her way, Helen accords Julia Severn's curls—and other human values—as little importance as Brocklehurst did. And if Helen's myth is no less narrow than Brocklehurst's, it is also no less complacently held.

Though her friend represents no solution to her contradictions, Jane nevertheless elevates Helen's death-wish into the heroism of a martyr. As the moon—a symbol which appears intermittently throughout the novel[19]— shines brightly on the two girls locked in an embrace, we note the familiar arrival of Jane's romantic imagination. The artist within her has once again simplified an ambiguous situation by infusing it with the intensity of illusion. It is not the last time that Jane will be vulnerable to the thrilling attractions of martyrdom.

Confronted throughout her life by the neatly dichotomized views of others, Jane can assert herself only by resisting these constructs. On many occasions after her imprisonment by the Reeds in the Red Room, she re-enacts her early means of defence: "I resisted all the way" (9). The tendency of those around her to find unambiguous solutions to life—and to force those solutions onto her—runs counter to Jane's very nature; unable either to synthesize her opposing inclinations into certainties or to find a satisfactory compromise, she can only refuse to act. Later in the novel she describes this pattern:

> I know no medium: I never in my life have known any medium in my dealings with positive, hard characters, antagonistic to my own, between absolute submission and determined revolt. I have always faithfully observed the one, up to the very moment of bursting, sometimes with volcanic vehemence, into the other.... (511)

This observation is one of many in which Jane shows herself to be both more forthright and more self-aware than either William Crimsworth or Lucy Snowe. For most of the novel, Jane has what both Brontë's other autobiographers and other characters in this novel lack: the virtue of her confusions. Though she is like a pendulum which is repeatedly arrested in mid-swing, she is at least partially conscious of the complexity of things. She knows what she cannot do. She cannot accept Rivers' plans for her, nor Rochester's, because she cannot contradict her own nature. Yet neither can she live peacefully with her contradictions. Particularly as the novel draws to its close, we note Jane's intense need to grasp some kind of reassuring certainty for herself.

IV. Rochester and Rivers: "Our Own Heaven Yonder"

Jane's most important relationship exists in that strange imaginative mid-region halfway between illusion and reality. The genesis of the relationship goes as far back as Gateshead. Enclosed in the Red Room, Jane is torn by opposition and dominated by her literary imagination. This time, as she looks at herself in the mirror, she has her own superstitions rather than Bewick for company:

> All looked colder and darker in that visionary hollow than in reality; and the strange little figure there gazing at me, with a white face and arms specking the gloom, and glittering eyes of fear moving where all else was still, had the effect of a real spirit: I thought it like one of the tiny phantoms, half fairy, half imp, Bessie's evening stories represented as coming up out of lone, ferny dells in moors, and appearing before the eyes of belated travellers. (12)

The image of herself as a fairy meeting travellers becomes actualized later when she first mets Rochester. As in earlier situations, she betrays her need to paint her life on the mythic canvas of aesthetic significance. This association of the Rochester relationship with the imaginative continues throughout their courtship. It is a relationship played out in a fairy setting: splitting chestnut trees, a murderous madwoman, and calls in the night are all part of its texture. Nowhere is Jane's Romantic sensibility, her need to transform life into fiction, more apparent.

Little Adèle commonsensically defines the nature of the relationship in her dialogue with Rochester about taking "'mademoiselle to the moon'" (335). After pointing out that the romantic world of fairyland does not necessarily ensure Jane of creature comforts ("'And her clothes, they will wear out: how can she get new ones?'" [336]), Adèle pins down the fundamental inadequacy of the couple's unworldly romance: "'besides, she would get tired of living with only you in the moon'" (336). Adèle in her wisdom sees that the endlessness of daydreams cannot be translated into the real world. As Jane both knows and does not know, the forever of fairy tales is both impossible and unsatisfying.

53

When Rochester enters her life accompanied by a Gytrash, Jane momentarily attempts to place him in the world of reality. She assures us that the human being's presence "broke the spell at once. Nothing ever rode the Gytrash . . ." (136). But Rochester's spell is never completely broken. His need to strike a Byronic pose—to utter fate-defying hyperbole, engage in cryptic dialogues, reminisce about his "'grande passion'"—dovetails perfectly with Jane's romantic vulnerability to heroes of "massive head," "granite-hewn features," "great dark eyes" (160). Despite her protestations of common sense, Jane is heavily committed to the fanciful quality of their relationship. As Jane Millgate has written of the early Rochester, "he is the product of two literary imaginations, his own and Jane's, both fully understood and controlled by the author."[20]

For Rochester, Jane is a talisman. She becomes, at various times, a "fairy," a "witch" or "sorceress," one of the "good genii," an "elf," someone from "the other world." Twice she is imaged as a "savage, beautiful" captive bird, "vivid, resolute," longing to soar (171, 405). All these references, of course, point to the illusory nature of the Jane who is created by her suitor. If Jane is struggling for a solution to the disequilibrium of her nature, Rochester is all too ready to provide an inadequate one. What he hopes to gain as he liberates his captive bird from the constraints of her past is nothing less than complete mastery of two fates. He wants to transform an imperfect world into a fairy place, and a separate soul into his reason for being.

If Jane is in danger of deluding herself through her imagination, however, she is by no means completely unaware. Her feelings about the relationship to Rochester, like her feelings about most things, are ambivalent. She confesses after the proposal, when Rochester begins to portray to her an image of the wealthy Mrs. Rochester, that "I really became uneasy at the strain he had adopted; because I felt he was either deluding himself, or trying to delude me" (326). As he insists that she give up governessing and promises to dress her in satin and lace, she begins to feel that her very identity is being threatened:

". . . I shall not be your Jane Eyre any longer, but an ape in a harlequin's jacket,—a jay in borrowed plumes." (326)

Even before she knows about Bertha, Jane becomes uncomfortable with the solution which Rochester offers her. The enclosures which figure the relationship—their "ring of golden peace" (309) and the proposal in the enclosed garden, for example—serve the same ambivalent function that they do in the other novels: they represent both security and confinement. But in

Jane's autobiography, unlike Crimsworth's, the ambivalent attitudes are not split between the reader and the narrator: Jane feels them both.

Behind Jane's doubts about her marriage is her lifelong inability to reconcile the claims of nature and grace. She worries about being overcommitted to earthly pleasures:

> My future husband was becoming to me my whole world; and, more than the world: almost my hope of heaven. He stood between me and every thought of religion, as an eclipse intervenes between man and the broad sun. I could not, in those days, see God for his creature: of whom I had made an idol. (346)

When she discovers the existence of Bertha, Jane finds her situation even more complicated. She recognizes that unambiguous action is impossible: conscience would have her stay with Rochester, and conscience would have her leave him. Once again, faced with the impossibility of a clear solution, Jane can only resist.

A similar ambivalence characterizes Jane's reaction to St. John Rivers. Like Rochester, Rivers becomes larger than life for Jane: he is both person and symbol, both real and illusory. Under Jane's shaping hand, the two men are made schematic opposites of each other. They are physically antithetical: St. John's handsome Greek face and fair complexion contrast with Rochester's dark and heavy visage. And Rivers' character, for Jane, is the perfect foil for Rochester's. One man espouses passion, the other claims the importance of higher moral pursuits. The dichotomy corresponds nicely to the divisions within Jane herself: each man speaks to half of her unsettled nature. But if Rochester offers to satisfy the needs of nature for Jane, and Rivers evokes her need for grace, neither presents her with a satisfying solution to her search. Like Rochester, Rivers finally threatens Jane's identity: "I was tempted to cease struggling with him—to rush down the torrent of his will into the gulf of his existence, and there lose my own" (534). Knowing "no medium," she can only assert herself by resisting him.

Jane does not immediately understand just what constitutes Rivers' myth. Her early responses to his feelings about Rosamond Oliver betray her misunderstanding. For quite some time, she reads the disequilibrium of her own nature into Rivers' suffering. St. John must explain to her that the anguish of deeply divided loyalties is not his problem:

> "It is strange," pursued he, "that while I love Rosamond Oliver so wildly —with all the intensity, indeed, of a first passion, the object of which is exquisitely beautiful, graceful, and fascinating—I experience at the same time a calm, unwarped consciousness, that she would not make me a good wife; that she is not the partner suited to me; that I should discover this

within a year after marriage; and that to twelve months' rapture would succeed a lifetime of regret. This I know." (476-77)

To this calm assertion of self-knowledge, Jane can only reply, "Strange, indeed!" And Jane's offer of Rosamond's portrait to St. John is another example of her confusion through vicarious identification. Certain that St. John needs emotional solace, she offers him the portrait—a physical image by which he can attempt (as Jane does with other portraits) to manipulate his feelings. But Rivers refuses the gift. Only slowly does Jane come to realize that the dynamics of her own emotions simply do not apply to Rivers.

When Jane does begin to establish some distance on Rivers, it is intellectual rather than emotional distance. By the time she admits that "I began to feel he had spoken truth of himself, when he said he was hard and cold" (501), she has lost most of her "liberty of mind":

> By degrees, he acquired a certain influence over me that took away my liberty of mind: his praise and notice were more restraining than his indifference. I could no longer talk or laugh freely when he was by; because a tiresomely importunate instinct reminded me that vivacity (at least in me) was distasteful to him. I was so fully aware that only serious moods and occupations were acceptable, that in his presence every effort to sustain or follow any other, became vain: I fell under a freezing spell. When he said "go," I went; "come," I came; "do this," I did it. But I did not love my servitude: I wished, many a time, he had continued to neglect me. (508)

Jane's servitude to Rivers echoes Rivers' servitude to his God: both have a strong need for a "Master," for a clearly defined myth by which to act with certainty. The difference between the two impulses lies in Jane's inability to yield fully to a monolith.

Jane's separateness from St. John is always tenuous and easily dissolved. Like Brocklehurst and Helen Burns (of whose natures he partakes), Rivers awakens a deeply-felt need. Though Jane cannot marry him, neither can she dismiss his call to her; having lost her "liberty of mind," she is even less able to understand Rivers' limitations than she was able to understand Helen's. Jane inflates Rivers, as she inflated Helen, into the epic proportions of a martyr: she sees him as one of nature's heroes. Although she claims to know his faults, she falls victim to his power. She cannot comprehend that, like Helen's, his repudiation of life for death is of questionable moral value. Nor does she recognize how fully he substitutes cold complacency for a generous comprehension of life's complexities. Jane will never overcome this vulnerability to Rivers. In her final presentation of her life's resolution, we see how strong is her inclination to emulate his servitude.

V. "Perfect Concord":
Jane's Insalubrious Eden

Jane's narrative of a complex lifetime of doubt is resolved by a single moment of epiphany. Although she asserts that Rochester's call makes everything clear for her, the reader has reason to wonder if her certainty was merely "the effect of excitement" (535). If ever a character were ready to be visited by a vision of clarity, it is Jane. Hectored by the missionary zeal of Rivers, she admits that "I was excited more than I had ever been" (535). Significantly, she hears the voice in a dim room which is "full of visions" and "full of moonlight." And if the reader has doubts, it is important to note that Jane, if only momentarily, has doubts of her own. As she hears the voice, she exorcises those doubts by force:

> "Down superstition!" I commented, as that spectre rose up black by the black yew at the gate. "This is not thy deception, nor thy witchcraft: it is the work of nature. She was roused, and did—no miracle—but her best." (536)

With the call in the night, nature and grace finally coalesce for Jane; she feels for the first time that her identity is secure: "It was *my* time to assume ascendancy. *My* powers were in play, and in force" (536). Proceeding to Ferndean and to "perfect concord" with Rochester, Jane claims to have found the answer to her uncertainties. For the first time, she feels sure about the path she has taken. Not only has she won the object of her love, but she has also been provided with a meaningful mission: she must spend the rest of her days caring for her blind and crippled husband. As she explains to Rochester, "'I love you better now, when I can really be useful to you, than I did in your state of proud independence, when you disdained every part but that of the giver and protector'" (570).

At the end of the novel Jane creates a tableau in which all the conflicting forces within her and within her world are resolved. Most critics have assumed that the resolution is Brontë's as well as Jane's, and have seen it as a convincingly-portrayed moral ideal.[21] Thus Robert Martin writes that "Jane and Rochester, learning to respect the inviolability of the soul as much as earthly delights, become a microcosm of man's striving for Christian reward."[22] And M. H. Scargill sums up the mediative quality of Jane's resolution in his description of her as "neither a profligate nor an ascetic, but a woman who has found an equable solution to the age-old problem...."[23] Indeed, life at Ferndean, for these critics, becomes a "lasting and durable paradise":

his [Rochester's] and Jane's reunion takes place against a benign background of profuse vegetation, and life-giving water bathes Ferndean when
she arrives. The name itself, meaning "fern valley"... supplies a bene-
diction connoting shelter and repose.[24]

a happy ending which even the most cynical critic cannot find inappro-
priate.... But this is a fortunate fall because she eventually re-enters...a
more lasting and durable paradise at Ferndean.[25]

... Miss Brontë never wrote a more sure and successful scene than this
reunion of lovers battered by life.... Like an echo of the end of *Paradise
Lost* they enter a new life, putting behind them the illicit Eden of the
garden at Thornfield, all forbidden passion spent.[26]

These critics rightly respond to the rich texture of Miltonic allusion in the
novel's final chapters. But the relationship of *Jane Eyre* to *Paradise Lost* is
perhaps more complicated than their comments would allow.[27]

In their rush to liken Ferndean to Milton's Eden, these critics have over-
looked the many ironies which Brontë has planted in Jane's paradise. The
Rochesters' Eden has as its setting a place so "insalubrious" that even Bertha
was not sent there. Ferndean is in an overgrown valley, with no sense of
prospect, "no opening anywhere" (550). The house in which Jane and
Rochester will live partakes of the confinement of the setting: "the windows
were latticed and narrow: the front-door was narrow, too..." (551). Compared to the ending of *Paradise Lost*, where the "world was all before"
Adam and Eve, this world is tightly enclosed, even claustrophobic. It is a
curious place indeed for a happy ending.[28]

Having struggled through dense foliage to Ferndean, Jane first sees Rochester as she stands in enclosed ground. Ferndean, like Thornfield, is an
illusory fairy-land. Ferndean's creatures, however, differ in one important
respect from the fairy and hero of the early novel: Jane and Rochester have
completely reversed their roles. The caged bird of earlier days is no longer
Jane, but Rochester;[29] the saviour who will attempt to liberate the bird, no
longer Rochester, but Jane. For Jane the new roles are a gratifying resolution: no longer subject to the humiliations of her "giver and protector," she
can assume the role herself: "prop and guide." The solution is not quite as
unambiguous as Jane supposes. The reader notes that Rochester, for example, whose sin was that he tried to make his own fate, now merely makes
Jane his fate: the difference is hardly substantive. And as Rochester's eyes,
Jane will not only interpret his world to him, she will thoroughly determine
his point of view. It is with skepticism about both of the lovers' futures that
we note this reversal of roles in Jane's latest form of enclosure: "... I ar-

rested his wandering hand, and prisoned it in both mine" (555). The bird is not caged, but prisoned; his keeper is his jailer. Neither will be set free.

If the fairy-tale has been turned upside-down, it has also been turned inside-out: the fanciful has become literal. What began as an imaginative construct—Jane's childish image in a mirror, which was filtered through Bessie's stories, enlarged by adolescent daydreams, and secured in portraits—is now completely a matter of the everyday. We wonder, as we contemplate the Rochesters' future, what Jane will *do* with herself at Ferndean, especially when we learn that Rochester is regaining his eyesight; not even noble self-sacrifice will be a lasting possibility for Jane. The chilling thought of day-to-day life at Ferndean brings to mind Adèle's early warning that Jane would tire of living on the moon with Rochester. We can only imagine Jane looking backward, not forward—trying to reconstruct, through her autobiography, a life that has nowhere else to go.

The dismal prospects of everyday life at Ferndean are intensified by the very force of Jane's protestations of unending bliss:

> I know no weariness of my Edward's society: he knows none of mine, any more than we each do of the pulsation of the heart that beats in our separate bosoms; consequently, we are ever together. To be together is for us to be at once as free as in solitude, as gay as in company. We talk, I believe, all day long: to talk to each other is but a more animated and an audible thinking. All my confidence is bestowed on him; all his confidence is devoted to me: we are precisely suited in character; perfect concord is the result. (576)

Jane's hyperbolic description of her happiness betrays the same complacency that she has confronted in other people so often. She speaks glibly on behalf of her husband; her repeated assertions that they are one have the effect of making Rochester disappear. And she also condescends to Rochester: as she "bestows" confidence on him, he "devotes" it to her. Characteristically, Jane attempts in this passage to make mythic what is ordinary—and in the process forces experience into a formula. But by means of her inflationary rhetoric, she inadvertently undercuts her own fictive Eden. The perfect concord she claims to have found is inconceivable outside the gates of Paradise.

Jane's new-found complacency extends to others besides Rochester. The attitudes she expresses at the end of her autobiography about the young Adèle, for example, sound disturbingly like the attitudes Mrs. Reed once held about the young Jane Eyre. Years earlier Mrs. Reed had been unable to summon regard for an "uncongenial alien":

> how could she really like an interloper not of her race, and unconnected with her, after her husband's death, by any tie? It must have been most

irksome to find herself bound by a hard-wrung pledge to stand in the stead of a parent to a strange child she could not love, and to see an uncongenial alien permanently intruded on her own family group. (14)

Although she seems to have become the model child that Jane never could be, Adèle is nevertheless being judged by the same cold standards:

As she grew up, a sound, English education corrected in a great measure her French defects; and when she left school, I found in her a pleasing and obliging companion: docile, good-tempered and well-principled. By her grateful attention to me and mine, she has long since well repaid any little kindness I ever had it in my power to offer her. (576)

Jane's self-satisfied condescension to the child echoes the bloodless attitude of her own first guardian; in becoming Mrs. Rochester, she has somehow dissolved into Mrs. Reed. Adèle's unfortunate situation delicately insinuates itself into Jane's happy ending.

Despite Jane's self-proclaimed sense of fulfillment, the final paragraphs of the novel reveal that her psychic equipoise is tentative. At centre stage when the story closes is not, as we might expect, the perfect concord of the Rochesters, but rather the zealous martyrdom of St. John Rivers. As Hunsden's physical presence disturbed the domestic tranquility of the Crimsworths, so Rivers' spiritual presence threatens Jane's peace. Jane's last words in her autobiography shatter her tone of pastoral contentment; while contemplating the fate of Rivers, she adopts his own frenetic idiom:

A more resolute, indefatigable pioneer never wrought amidst rocks and dangers. Firm, faithful, and devoted; full of energy, and zeal, and truth, he labours for his race: he clears their painful way to improvement; he hews down like a giant the prejudices of creed and caste that encumber it. He may be stern; he may be exacting; he may be ambitious yet: but his is the sternness of the warrior Greatheart, who guards his pilgrim-convoy from the onslaught of Apollyon. His is the exaction of the apostle, who speaks but for Christ, when he says—"Whosoever will come after me, let him deny himself, and take up his cross and follow me." His is the ambition of the high master-spirit, which aims to fill a place in the first rank of those who are redeemed from the earth—who stand without fault before the throne of God; who share the last mighty victories of the lamb; who are called, and chosen, and faithful. (578)

Jane's imagination is ignited by Rivers' grand commitment and by his absolute certainty of the path he has taken. Something within her compares the epic scale of Rivers' mission with her pedestrian existence at Ferndean and an abyss of uncertainty opens before her—despite her protestations to the contrary. When she notes that in the hour of Rivers' death, "his mind will be unclouded; his heart will be undaunted; his hope will be sure; his faith

60

steadfast" (578-79), Jane attributes to him the certainty which she has always desired. We realize that life at Ferndean will not provide this certainty. If she has finally gained control of two lives, Jane can hardly master her own emotional equilibrium. Like William Crimsworth, she has transformed her outer life—but her inner life remains as unsettled as it has always been.

The sense of satisfying closure which Jane claims in her autobiography's final chapters, then, is qualified by the reader's sense of her claustrophobia. For rather than beginning her life at Ferndean, she seems to be living her death instead. Nothing remains for her to do with herself. She can only revitalize a static life by writing it; she can only attempt a resurrection by turning to autobiography.

The autobiography she produces, however, seems to be something that was conceived on Thornfield's third story. We recall her earlier remarks:

> my sole relief was to walk along the corridor of the third story, backwards and forwards . . . and allow my mind's eye to dwell on whatever bright visions rose before it . . . and, best of all, to open my inward ear to a tale that was never ended—a tale my imagination created, and narrated continuously. . . . (132)

Walking backwards and forwards along the corridor of her life, Jane has created one of her elevated tales that never ended. She has settled finally for the easy complacency of a myth predicated on happy endings. And as Brontë implies, such happy endings occur only in fiction—in imaginary, prelapsarian worlds which are unacquainted with life's unavoidable ambiguity. Through her art, Jane has deluded herself. For the sake of a narrow clarity, she has clung to her "bright visions," forsaken her keen awareness of complexity. If Jane Eyre needs her clarity, however, Charlotte Brontë does not let it stand unqualified. She answers Jane's unworldly fiction with her own severe Truth. At the last moment, as Jane thinks of Rivers from Ferndean, an uninvited visitor seems to intrude into the carefully arranged chamber of her mind: Jane is not in fact free from either doubt or desire. Brontë implies that the last door will remain ajar; Jane cannot lock up her truth in fiction.

CHAPTER FOUR

Villette

The superficial similarities between Brontë's first novel and her last have prompted many readers to consider *Villette* as a revision of *The Professor*. It is certainly true that in *Villette* Brontë returned to some of the material that she had explored many years earlier: both novels take place in continental girls' schools where teachers, directresses, and their complicated liaisons figure prominently. It is also true that in her last novel Brontë returned (after having used a third-person narrator in *Shirley*) to the form of fictional autobiography. But *Villette* and *The Professor* must not be thought of as two drafts of the same novel. To return, for Brontë, was not to repeat. As we have seen with both *Jane Eyre* and *The Professor*, the essential nature of a fictional autobiography derives from the character of its autobiographer. And Lucy Snowe is very unlike her predecessors.

Just as William Crimsworth sought refuge in his strait and secret nook and Jane Eyre remained vulnerably defensive in her unlocked room, so Lucy Snowe has her characteristic mode of enclosure. Early in the novel she describes this mode: ". . . I had a staid manner of my own which ere now had been as good to me as cloak and hood of hodden grey. . . ."[1] Unlike the enclosures of her predecessors, Lucy's is a portable one; wherever she goes, she lurks mysteriously within the disguise of her cloak and hood. And with disdainful recalcitrance, she resists our attempts to clarify her nature. Perhaps because Lucy presents such a defiant challenge, critics have been more willing with *Villette* than with the earlier novels to recognize the distance between the narrator and Charlotte Brontë.[2] But although *Villette* has escaped the worst excesses of biographical interpretation, its significance as fictional autobiography remains to be explored. Paradoxically, it is by examining Lucy's disguise—the contours of her self-portrait—that we can begin to establish the identity of the person who hides beneath the cloak and hood.

The problem of Lucy's identity baffles her acquaintances as much as it vexes her reader.[3] Characteristically, she gives no answer to Polly's question, which comes late in the novel:

"Lucy, I wonder if anybody will ever comprehend you altogether?" (387)

But clearly Lucy enjoys having the question asked, both by Polly and by her reader. Indeed, she fills her autobiography with images and situations which elicit questions about her identity. Time and again she faces mirrors which reflect her plainness, her suffering, her differences from others, her view of herself. And just as she keeps before us her image as it is reflected to herself, so she also dwells on her image as it is perceived by others. Thus in Graham's eyes, we are told, she is "'a being inoffensive as a shadow'" (289). To Mrs. Bretton, she is "'my wise, dear, grave little god-daughter'" (248). And lest we lose sight of the chameleon which represents Lucy-as-seen-by-her-world (-as-seen-by-Lucy), we are given an occasional summary:

> What contradictory attributes of character we sometimes find ascribed to us, according to the eye with which we are viewed! Madame Beck esteemed me learned and blue; Miss Fanshawe, caustic, ironic, and cynical; Mr. Home, a model teacher, the essence of the sedate and discreet: somewhat conventional, perhaps, too strict, limited, and scrupulous, but still the pink and pattern of governess-correctness; whilst another person, Professor Paul Emanuel to wit, never lost an opportunity of intimating his opinion that mine was rather a fiery and rash nature—adventurous, indocile, and audacious. I smiled at them all. (274-75)

Lucy's condescending smile is no doubt aimed also at her reader.

Having raised the question of her identity so obtrusively, Lucy takes great pains to prevent us from answering it. Time and again in her autobiography she withholds crucial information about herself, teasing the reader with veiled references to her experience. The liberties she takes with her autobiographical material far surpass those of Jane Eyre and William Crimsworth. About her past life she keeps us in the dark; aside from shadowy allusions to three experiences with death, to family dissolution, to "single-handed conflict with Life, with Death, with Grief, with Fate" (159), she tells us nothing. She is equally coy about the present. The reader's imagination is not invited to picture her narrating her story; there is no counterpart to Crimsworth at Daisy Lane nor to Jane at Ferndean. The only reference, in fact, to Lucy's current situation is the "snow beneath snow" image by which she describes her white hair and cap (37). And she continues to leave questions unanswered throughout the autobiography. At many points, poised on the edge of a revelation, she withdraws into secrecy. Thus we never discover what she confesses to Père Silas, nor in what play Vashti performs, nor with what reassurances Paul Emanuel soothes his lover's fears. Lucy's need for her pose of enigmatic autobiographer is made apparent when she says of Dr. John: "I liked entering his presence covered with a cloud he had not seen through . . ." (157). Ginevra articulates the reader's problem as well as her own when she asks repeatedly, "'Who *are* you, Miss Snowe?'" (280).

Lucy's answer to Ginevra—"'Perhaps a personage in disguise'" (280)—suggests the extent of her elusiveness. In referring to herself as a personage—a term which is associated not only with figures of social importance but also with fictionalized characters—she hints at what defines her as a narrator. Lucy prefers to approach her life as a construct, and herself as an aesthetic creation. Beneath her cloak and hood is a series of poses, a second line of defence against our attempts to penetrate her disguise. With playful aggressiveness she plants evidence, dangles hints—and always dodges definitions. The creator never quite lets us know the sufferer. Considering that her desire to withhold often seems much stronger than her desire to tell, we wonder what prompted her to write her life story at all.

Lucy's reliance on abstractions is a good example of her posing. We have noted in both Jane Eyre and William Crimsworth a tendency to describe their inner conflicts in terms of moral categories. For Lucy Snowe Abstraction is so essential that it becomes a veritable Autobiographic Muse. Truth, Falsehood, Reason, Feeling, Imagination, Freedom, Renovation, Will, Power —Lucy's list of abstractions surpasses even Crimsworth's. She separates her inclinations into two camps—most often Imagination and Reason—and portrays her life as a pitched battle between the two. Lucy's fights between abstractions, however, always seem thrown in advance. When she castigates "This hag, this Reason" and cheers on "Imagination—*her* soft, bright foe, *our* sweet Help, our divine Hope" (207) only to reverse her position some ten pages later (Imagination becomes "a mess of that manna I drearily eulogised a while ago" [217]), we question whether she has undergone a real transformation. Lucy relies on abstractions as part of her disguise; partly they distance the reader from her final commitment and partly they simplify the issues for her. The smooth moral surfaces she attempts to create for herself by means of her abstractions are explained by Jean Frantz Blackall as "the philosophic and religious formulae that she invokes to sustain her in the face of the contradictory evidence of experience."[4] Lucy presents her life as a series of inner moral conflicts. But the final victors in these conflicts are always less important than the spectacle of the battles themselves.

To a much greater extent than with Jane Eyre or William Crimsworth, we also note the contrivance of Lucy's narrative technique. Her language provides an example. By inverting sentence patterns ("I know not" [1]; "'Of what are these things the signs and tokens?'" [2]; "whose shadow I scarce guessed" [2]), by cultivating deliberately archaic expressions ("esteemed it a grievous pity" [1]; "explanations ensued" [2]), and by suddenly arresting her narrative with such pedantic devices as "Imprimis" (72), Lucy attains a self-consciously formal idiom which makes Jane Eyre's style seem almost unpremeditated. Nor could Jane have risen to Lucy's carefully controlled shifts in point of view ("Cancel the whole of that, if you please, reader" [48])—a device which she uses a number of times in her narrative. The plot itself is engineered so deliberately that at times it seems pure contrivance. The episode with Miss Marchmont tidily foreshadows Lucy's doom and usefully reflects her maxims:

> "O my noble Frank—my faithful Frank—my *good* Frank! so much better than myself—his standard in all things so much higher! This I can now see and say: if few women have suffered as I did in his loss, few have enjoyed what I did in his love. It was a far better kind of love than common; I had no doubts about it or him: it was such a love as honoured, protected, and elevated, no less than it gladdened her to whom it was given. Let me now ask . . . let me reflect why it was taken from me? For what crime was I condemned, after twelve months of bliss, to undergo thirty years of sorrow? . . . We should acknowledge God merciful, but not always for us comprehensible. We should accept our own lot, whatever it be, and try to render happy that of others." (32-34)

And finally, the coincidences of the plot—Lucy's arbitrary discovery of Madame Beck's Pensionnat, the reunion of Homes and Brettons in Villette, the second incarnation of Polly's and Graham's love, the Père Silas connection, the lechers who turn out to be Professors—are more striking than in either of the earlier novels. Though he should have levelled his remarks at Lucy Snowe rather than at Charlotte Brontë, we can readily sympathize with David Cecil's complaint that "She stretches the long arm of coincidence till it becomes positively dislocated."[5]

We cannot trust Lucy Snowe. As she writes her autobiography, she does not, like William Crimsworth, naïvely attempt to extract a moral message for her reader. Nor does she, like Jane Eyre, forthrightly admit to shaping her tale in the interest of coherence. Dangling ghosts before her readers with the full knowledge that she is duping us, Lucy is capable of a kind of artistic manipulation to which neither the obtuse William Crimsworth nor the four-square Jane Eyre could have stooped. Yet despite the deliberate contrivances of her narrative, Lucy does not manage to remain as opaque as she would hope. As both an observer and a participant in her own story, Lucy partakes of the paradox of the artist whose material is himself. We see her just as she at one point describes herself: "Half in earnest, half in seeming" (293).

I. Lucy as Looker-On

I acted to please myself. (126)

As we would expect with so self-conscious a narrator, the quality of artifice which we noted in *Jane Eyre*—the sense that life was merging with art—is in *Villette* pushed to its extreme. In this monument to craft, we recognize not the milestones of a life, but the artifacts of a dominating imagination. Indeed, art and artifice so thoroughly inform *Villette* that even Jane Eyre's careful shaping of her life seems ingenuous by comparison. But Lucy's mode as artist differs markedly from that of Jane and Crimsworth. We recall that the visual arts were most important to the earlier narrators. William Crimsworth framed pictures: by this means he arranged his readings of the world into gratifying compositions. Jane Eyre, on the other hand, painted pictures: as externalizations of her emotional struggles, they offered her relief and consolation. Lucy, however—though she sometimes describes people as paintings and though she is the only narrator who actually visits a gallery—seems not to have the kind of imagination which is captured by paintings. Whether it be the fleshy Cleopatra or the drab "La vie d'une femme," no painting ever thoroughly engages her. About them all she insistently asks the wrong kind of question and makes inappropriately narrow moral judgments. Her unaesthetic reactions, however, are not without an ample measure of self-awareness. Of the Cleopatra she says:

> She lay half-reclined on a couch: why, it would be difficult to say; broad daylight blazed round her: she appeared in hearty health, strong enough to do the work of two plain cooks; she could not plead a weak spine; she ought to have been standing, or at least sitting bolt upright. She had no business to lounge away the noon on a sofa. (180)

Lucy's tone verges on self-parody; her mischievous remarks reveal an emotional disengagement with the painting. This painting, like others, is perceived by Lucy as an unconvincing form of pretend; she will not play the game.

Lucy's artistic medium is the drama. Her one experience on the stage (in Paul Emanuel's school play) elicits, unlike paintings, both her total engagement and her passionate vitality. At no other point in the novel does the always calculating Lucy become spontaneous:

> What I felt that night, and what I did, I no more expected to feel and do, than to be lifted in a trance to the seventh heaven. Cold, reluctant, apprehensive, I had accepted a part to please another: ere long, warming, becoming interested, taking courage, I acted to please myself. (126)

But the experience threatens as it reveals; her discomfort with it is made clear by her immediate and final renunciation of the stage:

> Yet the next day, when I thought it over, I quite disapproved of these amateur performances; and though glad that I had obliged M. Paul, and tried my own strength for once, I took a firm resolution never to be drawn into a similar affair. A keen relish for dramatic expression had revealed itself as part of my nature; to cherish and exercise this new-found faculty might gift me with a world of delight, but it would not do for a mere looker-on at life: the strength and longing must be put by; and I put them by, and fastened them in with the lock of a resolution which neither Time nor Temptation has since picked. (126)

Lucy is determined not to be an actor on life's stage, but rather to be a looker-on. The questions which we have seen her pose about who she is have finally been rhetorical; she has long ago decided what her role will be. She will be a spectator—one who sits in shadowy recesses, clad in her costume/disguise, and looks out upon the acting of others; her desire for other roles has been locked away.

Although Lucy has renounced acting, she has not given up the stage. Her visit to the theatre to see the performance of Vashti is an experience of great significance to her, marked with a "deep-red cross" in her "book of life" (236). Vashti's performance summons from Lucy the passionate involvement that was lacking at the picture gallery. Like her part in the school play, it "drew my heart out of its wonted orbit..." (235). She attempts, rather half-heartedly, to place a reductive moral valuation on Vashti's performance; yet as we know from her language, it is finally not as a "spectacle low, horrible, immoral" but as "a mighty revelation" (234) that Vashti's acting most impresses her. So complete is Lucy's engagement in the drama that her remarks become at times almost unintelligible; the coolly amused condescension she felt for the Cleopatra has vanished.

Lucy is unable to keep distinct the boundaries between the actress and the character she portrays. We cannot be certain—when Vashti is first called a natural force (a "planet" [233]), then quickly becomes a "chaos" (234), and then is "something neither of woman nor of man: in each of her eyes sat a devil" (234)—just when Lucy is referring to the character and when to the actress. Her castigation of Dr. John's "callous" "branding judgment" (236) of the woman is ironic: Lucy's own responses are not purely aesthetic. She has become involved in a deeply personal way with Vashti's performance.

Lucy finds much in Vashti to identify with. As a woman who has refused to expose herself to what she considers the vulgar masses, the Biblical queen[6] is much more like the unexposed Lucy than was that "slug" (235), the

Cleopatra. (We recall that Cleopatra, even with her seven-and-twenty yards of material, could not manage to make a decent garment for herself. Certainly she would have had no interest in a protective covering like Lucy's.) Lucy's sadistic daydream of Cleopatra's "pulpy mass" (235) being cut through by Vashti is a good indication of where her emotional proclivities lie.

Although Lucy is transfixed by Vashti's implicit similarity to herself, the actress on stage is vastly different from the looker-on in the audience. For if Vashti has refused one kind of exposure (in denying her husband's request), she welcomes another. Unlike Lucy, Vashti is not emotionally self-protective; she rebels against her Fate, takes her place defiantly on the stage of her life, and reveals her suffering openly: "To her, what hurts becomes immediately embodied: she looks on it as a thing that can be attacked, worried down, torn in shreds" (234). Most of Lucy's intense reaction to the performance, then, comes from vicarious participation in what she is herself unable to do. The many references in the Vashti passage that figure violently erupting emotion—"lava" (234), the "swollen winter river thundering in cataract" (235), the "tigress" who "rends her woes" (234)—represent what Lucy has put by, but what must, for that very reason, speak deeply to her. Vashti is for Lucy the road not taken; the self-declared looker-on has deliberately sealed off the Vashti within her.

Implicit in Lucy's renunciation of acting is her renunciation of purposive action. Indeed, her language betrays her as the heroine of the passive verb. Preparing to leave the confines of Miss Marchmont's sick-room, she tells us that "It seemed I must be stimulated into action. I must be goaded, driven, stung, forced to energy" (31). Similarly, as she reflects on her first evening in Villette, she declares, "Strangely had I been led since morning—unexpectedly had I been provided for" (59). Again and again Lucy uses such constructions to refer to herself; and the force which goads, stings, leads, and provides is, of course, Lucy's constant, almost palpable, companion—Fate itself. So total is her investment in Fate that she assigns it a large measure of responsibility for the most substantial, and the most trivial, events in her life. For her devastating nervous illness during the school holiday, Lucy shares the guilt with Fate. When Dr. John asks "'Who is in the wrong, then, Lucy?'" she replies, "'Me—Dr. John—me; and a great abstraction on whose wide shoulders I like to lay the mountains of blame they were sculptured to bear: me and Fate'" (167). Later, Fate appoints her the role of go-between for the young lovers and Mr. Home: "Invested by fate with the part of confidante and mediator, I was obliged to go on" (389). And Fate is the lonely culprit behind Lucy's inability to produce Paul Emanuel's watch-guard at the appropriate moment: "I had meant to gratify him. Fate would not have it so" (311).

The passive verbs of Lucy's language reflect a sensibility which waits to be guided. She claims that the "[t]wo hot, close rooms" which were her "world" at Miss Marchmont's would have remained her world, even for twenty years more (30-31), had Fate not decreed otherwise. And she makes the same remark later, as she is catapulted by Madame Beck out of the nursery and into the schoolroom. "If left to myself, I should infallibly have let this chance slip. Inadventurous, unstirred by impulses of practical ambition, I was capable of sitting twenty years teaching infants the hornbook, turning silk dresses, and making children's frocks" (66). Lucy is not claiming, as she makes quite clear, that she was particularly happy, or even content, in either of her early situations. But happiness, after all, is not something one cultivates: "Happiness is not a potato, to be planted in mould, and tilled with manure" (227). So fixed is Lucy's idea of her place in the scheme of things that pushing Fate—even slightly nudging it—would be out of the question.

At many points in her narrative, Lucy's passivity in the face of unfolding experience seems gratuitous, or even perverse, to the reader. Early in the novel she meets an old schoolmate, but makes no effort to recall herself to the woman. A number of times she observes Madame Beck rifling through her belongings and does not comment. But her most remarkable reticences, of course, occur with Dr. John. For some time she will not divulge that she has recognized him (even to the reader), and she never mentions to him their chance meeting on her first night in Villette. Lucy is intractable in her refusal to exploit opportunities through her own initiative. She prefers to lurk about on the periphery of things, "a mere looker-on at life," enjoying her role as a pawn in Fate's game. At home in her "gown of shadows," considering herself "a mere shadowy spot on a field of light" (116), she retreats into the folds of her cloak and hood.

Lucy's willingness to be led by Fate, however, is often ironic. By abdicating one kind of control over her life, she is in fact exercising another. She is well aware, for example, by the time that the school holiday arrives, that people on whom she has a long-standing claim are living close by. Yet rather than take the initiative of contacting the Brettons, she chooses to endure the most agonizing suffering she has ever encountered. Indeed, up to that time she has not even recalled herself to Graham: "To *say* anything on the subject, to *hint* at my discovery, had not suited my habits of thought, or assimilated with my system of feeling" (157). Lucy's "habits of thought" and "system of feeling" do not exempt her from the charge of interfering in her destiny; she is simply interfering in her own way. We know from the beginning of the story, when Lucy finds young Polly's demonstrations of affection for Graham "strangely rash" (22), that she is a person who fears the slightest kind of emotional risk-taking. We observe her trying to fend off her needs for affection from the Brettons by scrupulously refusing to cultivate their friendship. But in insisting on passivity, she is shaping her life quite emphatically. Even when she is on the brink of losing Paul Emanuel to Guadaloupe and the Catholic junta, she will not act:

> To follow, to seek out, to remind, to recall—for these things I had no faculty.
> M. Emanuel might have passed within reach of my arm: had he passed silent and unnoticing, silent and stirless should I have suffered him to go by. (403)

To a great extent Lucy makes her Fate by accepting it.

From time to time other characters in the novel become Fate surrogates for Lucy. As Mrs. Bretton organizes Lucy's dressing for an evening at the theatre (187) or Graham interrogates her about her ghostly visitation (225), we note Lucy's characteristic docility in the hands of those who guide with certainty. She is most comfortable, and most energetic, with people who assume the responsibility for her actions. Her relationship to Madame Beck is a striking example of this inclination to be led. From Lucy's vantage point, "Destiny and Madame Beck seemed in league" (85). The schoolmistress is able to inspire in her perhaps the strongest commitment she makes—the commitment to her teaching career. As Lucy describes her first entry into the classroom, she speaks of Madame Beck with the passive constructions she uses to speak of Fate: "my hand was taken into hers, and I was conducted downstairs" (67):

> I might have ... gone back to nursery obscurity, and there, perhaps, mouldered for the rest of my life; but looking up at Madame, I saw in her countenance a something that made me think twice ere I decided. At that instant she did not wear a woman's aspect, but rather a man's. Power of a particular kind strongly limned itself in all her traits, and that power was not *my* kind of power: neither sympathy, nor congeniality, nor submission, were the emotions it awakened. I stood—not soothed, nor won, nor overwhelmed. It seemed as if a challenge of strength between opposing gifts was given, and I suddenly felt all the dishonour of my diffidence, all the pusillanimity of my slackness to aspire. (67)

Finally, as we shall see later, Paul Emanuel, Lucy's fiery schoolmaster, elicits through his tyranny her greatest determination to act. About her need for intellectual accomplishments, Lucy maintains: "when M. Paul sneered at me, I wanted to possess them more fully: his injustice stirred in me ambitious wishes—it imparted a strong stimulus—it gave wings to aspiration" (320).

Behind Lucy Snowe's strident fatalism is a carefully-conceived personal mythology. Her "habits of thought" and "system of feeling" place her neatly within a rigid moral framework. Time and again in her narrative she alludes to her conviction that her destiny has been immutably determined:

> With what dread force the conviction would grasp me that Fate was my permanent foe, never to be conciliated. I did not, in my heart, arraign the mercy or justice of God for this; I concluded it to be a part of His great plan that some must deeply suffer while they live, and I thrilled in the certainty that of this number I was one. (141)

Lucy sees herself as a member of an unfortunate Elect. Rotating the Calvinist moon to its darker side, she isolates two groups of chosen ones, the fortunate few who are

> so born, so reared, so guided from a soft cradle to a calm and late grave, that no excessive suffering penetrates their lot, and no tempestuous blackness overcasts their journey. And often these are not pampered, selfish beings, but Nature's elect, harmonious and benign; men and women mild with charity, kind agents of God's kind attributes (397)

and, on the other hand, the lookers-on, the Lucy Snowes, who are not shut out from God's mercy, but must wait for the afterlife to experience it.[7] Members of the unfortunate elect have drawn lives of unmitigated pain in God's inscrutable lottery. So certain is Lucy of her place in the scheme of things that her prophecy can only become self-fulfilling.

Every autobiographer is his own spectator, but Lucy Snowe casts an unusually cold eye on her reconstructed image. She enters the book with a prepared thesis about herself; her efforts to maintain the thesis are as dogged as they are self-conscious. Aware of herself as a "personage," she occasionally establishes a surprising distance on the person she claims to have been. When she speaks of herself reading Dr. John's letter in the attic, for example, she suddenly switches to the third person:

> The poor English teacher in the frosty garret, reading by a dim candle guttering in the wintry air, a letter simply good-natured—nothing more. ... (221)

As this passage implies, Lucy's autobiography is her theatre; as director, she manipulates not only the characters around her, but her own interpreted image as well. Having approved the script, she sets her own stage and then casts herself with determination in the role she has created. Behind her careful efforts to stage-manage her autobiography lies Lucy's constant awareness of what she refers to as "surface":

> it is on the surface only the common gaze will fall. As to what lies below, leave that with God. (161)

Lucy quite deliberately cultivates her surface in order to attract—and deflect—the common gaze. As character and autobiographer, she is most comfortable with her facade; she would prefer that the backstage workings of her theatre not be explored. She admits to us many times that she has created a placid exterior for her acquaintances. We know as well that as readers we are often kept at a distance. What is less obvious, perhaps, is Lucy's determination to forestall her own self-scrutiny. No one—whether it be her associates, her reader, or, most importantly, herself—must penetrate her carefully-wrought disguise. Any doubts she may have—about her view of Lucy Snowe, about her autobiographical purposes, or about the self beneath the pose—she prefers to leave with God. Her autobiography adumbrates that preference.

II.   Lucy's Procrustean Bed

"a tale of ambitious proportions, and the spectacle of the narrator sticking fast in the midst" (369)

a mere network reticulated with holes (407)

Many people in *Villette* are called by a variety of names. Ginevra's list of nicknames for Lucy is even longer than Mr. Home's impressive list of titles; the acquired designations of John Graham Bretton are only slightly more numerous than the names which "P.C.D.E." was given at birth. If it is true, as Tristram Shandy's father so convincingly declared, that names shape people more than people shape names, the obverse is likewise possible: ambiguities in naming point to ambiguities in people. Identifying and understanding, in a world where names multiply, become relative matters; character resides not in the person being described, but in the describer. To a certain extent, the world of *Villette* suffers from the Biblical affliction of confounded language.[8] Both in its literal bilingualism and in its less obvious confusions about names,[9] Villette is a world in which people do not understand each other: they lack a common vocabulary.

Yet if the characters in the novel suffer from a confusion of tongues, their eyesight is even more seriously confounded. Unlike St. Lucy, who heals those with visual problems, Lucy Snowe presides over a world of astigmatism. As Madame Beck peers through her keyholes, Paul Emanuel spies through his magic lattice, and Père Silas glances obliquely at Lucy, we recognize that the deeper affliction in the novel is not one of speaking but rather one of seeing. In *Villette* Lucy has created a world in which eyes are the primary threat: espionage directs people's actions; eyes conceal rather than reflect their meanings; and, most important, eyes represent a constant and almost palpable invasion of privacy. As we have noted, Lucy's first fear is of being seen through; it is not surprising that she finds other people's eyes so menacing. But spying is also her own mode: by her determination, she exists in order to look on. Glancing out from her shadowy recesses, Lucy's predatory eyes find many unsuspecting victims. As we turn our attention to some of the novel's other characters, we begin to note distortions in Lucy's way of looking.

For the most part Lucy shapes other characters in the autobiography to fit her personal mythology. Graham and Polly are useful evidence for Lucy of her tidy view of the cosmos. The perfect counterparts of her own plight, they represent the "soft cradle to late grave" elect. Graham, we are told, "was born victor as some are born vanquished" (395):

> Dr. John himself was one of those on whose birth benign planets have certainly smiled. Adversity might set against him her most sullen front: he was the man to beat her down with smiles. Strong and cheerful, and firm and courteous; not rash, yet valiant; he was the aspirant to woo Destiny herself, and to win from her stone eyeballs a beam almost loving. (159)

And Polly rises in Lucy's estimation after she has become Graham's chosen partner:

> "Providence has protected and cultured you, not only for your own sake, but I believe for Graham's. His star, too, was fortunate: to develop fully the best of his nature, a companion like you was needed: there you are, ready. You must be united. I knew it the first day I saw you together at La Terrasse. In all that mutually concerns you and Graham there seems to me promise, plan, harmony." (343)

But the problem with Lucy's assessment of Graham and Polly is that ultimately she must do some wrenching in order to fit them into her scheme. Her description of their subsequent married life is appalling:

> This pair was blessed indeed, for years brought them, with great prosperity, great goodness: they imparted with open hand, yet wisely. Doubtless they knew crosses, disappointments, difficulties; but these were well borne. More than once, too, they had to look on Him whose face flesh scarce can see and live: they had to pay their tribute to the King of Terrors. In the fulness of years, M. de Bassompierre was taken: in ripe old

age departed Louisa Bretton. Once even there rose a cry in their halls, of Rachel weeping for her children; but others sprang healthy and blooming to replace the lost. . . . (398)

Using images of natural process ("ripe," "blooming"), Lucy imposes an interpretation on the Brettons' deaths which deprives them of their sting. Worst of all, her trivialization of the death of Graham and Polly's child— who, she implies, was easy to "replace"—is chilling in an almost Crimsworthian fashion. In order to use Graham and Polly as foils for her own destiny, Lucy has reduced their future to a formula. So great is her need to attest to the "promise, plan, harmony" of the Brettons' life that she distorts their tragedy into paradigmatic domestic bliss.

Many characters in the novel are similarly distorted by the perceiving eyes of Lucy Snowe. The self-professed "looker-on at life" becomes a self-betrayed voyeur;[10] her "distorting involvement"[11] with the people she describes reflects ironically on her own limitations. Lucy's discussion of young Polly in the early pages of the novel reveals this voyeurism in its purest form. With the detachment of an anthropologist observing an alien race, she claims to enjoy "the amusement of this study of character" (23). She proceeds to "take notice" of and chronicle every move that little Polly (pejoratively called "this being," a "doll," "the creature," "minute thing") makes. From her shadowy corner, Lucy watches the child praying, playing, dressing, weeping, and suffering in silence. Her interest in Polly, of course, is more than that of the excessively curious onlooker. She is morbidly and jealously resentful of Polly. At a time when Polly needs consolation, Lucy allows her to cry herself to sleep. Frequently she censors Polly for indulging in natural emotional responses ("I often wished she would mind herself and be tranquil" [18]; "One would have thought the child had no mind or life of her own" [19]; "Candidly speaking, I thought her a little busy-body" [10]). Lucy is sarcastic about Polly's relationship with her father and angry about her devotion to Graham. Worst of all, she deliberately engineers situations in order to watch Polly suffer. Thus she first encourages Polly to interrupt Graham's party and then, after the inevitable rejection, attempts to console the child with "maxims of philosophy" (20). The cool detachment from Polly which Lucy claims to feel is unconvincing. As Terry Eagleton explains, "Lucy's attitude to Polly is, in fact, a subconscious tactical conversion of suppressed jealousy to mature condescension; a sort of malice is rationalised as a briskly commonsensical taking in hand."[12]

Behind her suppressed rage at Polly is an inability on Lucy's part to handle her own emotions. Her frequent discomfort at the expression of natural affection or natural grief betrays inadequately realized psychic needs, "coldly unacknowledged impulses."[13] So involved does she become with Polly's feelings that by the end of the child's stay in the Bretton house Lucy has begun to confuse Polly's identity with her own. When she counsels Polly to cultivate callousness toward Graham, she is projecting her own emotional vulnerability onto someone else. Although she speaks about Polly when she asks,

> "How will she get through this world, or battle with this life? How will she bear the shocks and repulses, the humiliations and desolations, which books, and my own reason, tell me are prepared for all flesh?" (28)

we realize that she is in fact voicing her personal fears. Lucy's cloaked self-protectiveness is not a sufficiently secure enclosure for the containment of her deep insecurities.

Such projections recur throughout the novel. Characters from whom Lucy distances herself by attitudes of scorn, indignation, or condescension, ironically appear to the reader as unexpurgated aspects of her own frustrated desires. As Lucy attempts to create characters who are inferior to herself, she inadvertently creates doubles.[14] Thus Ginevra Fanshawe, the shallow antitype to Lucy's puritanical self-image and the recipient of most of Lucy's moralistic sermonizing, is also the only resident of the Pensionnat with whom Lucy will share food. Their strange bond is reinforced during the school holiday when Ginevra suddenly becomes a heroine in Lucy's tortured mind. As the boundaries between Lucy and Ginevra somehow dissolve, the invitation to see Ginevra as a suppressed part of Lucy is hard to resist. Similarly, Madame Beck—Lucy's prototype of the spying, deceitful, and tyrannical schoolmistress—is only a more competent practitioner of Lucy's own skills.[15] (Indeed, when we observe Lucy's capacity for brutal insensitivity as she laughs with Dr. John about the older woman's infatuation, we even begin to wonder which of the two women is in fact the more heartless.) So ambiguous are the boundaries between Lucy and the characters she creates that the crétin (141), whose propensity for evil so disgusts and wearies her keeper, becomes a figure for the dark underside of Lucy's own psyche, over which she keeps a similarly constant vigil. Even Sylvie the dog, who enjoys Paul Emanuel's caresses and invites "affection by her beauty and her vivacious life" (379), is an unwitting recipient of Lucy's wish-fulfillment. It is difficult to imagine that Brontë's ironic rendering of Lucy Snowe could have been done with more delicacy or power. As Inga-Stina Ewbank has written, "it is the probings into the deprivations of the heart and into the neuroses of its owner which make the novel into what must be one of the greatest psychological novels in English in the nineteenth century."[16]

Only one character in *Villette* seems free from the distorting involvement of Lucy's perceiving eye. Paul Emanuel is annexed by neither Lucy the character nor Lucy the autobiographer; his point of view, as much as his attitude to Catholicism, is thoroughly separate. The vulnerability of Lucy's disguise to the piercing eye of Paul is evident during their first encounter: "A resolute compression of the lips and gathering of the brow seemed to say that he meant to see through me, and that a veil would be no veil for him" (57). We know that Paul does indeed penetrate Lucy's disguise when, to Madame Beck's question, "'May one trust her word?'" he warily replies, "'Are you negotiating a matter of importance?'" (57). Considering Lucy's guileful ways, such a first impression is perceptive indeed. It is not surprising that, reversing the usual situation, Paul forces Lucy to act in his play; the narrator's own well-defined drama of her life will not quite accommodate his independence. Through Paul Emanuel, Brontë adjusts the reader's perspective on the novel's governing consciousness: he helps us see through Lucy's surface.

Paul Emanuel is in, but not of, the deceitful and claustrophobic world of Villette.[17] Like others in the novel, he is responsible for confining Lucy—but in locking her into the attic, he is encouraging the looker-on to become an actor. Like others in the novel, he spies—but he peers at Lucy through transparent windows, making no effort to conceal his genuine concern. Like others in the novel, he interferes—but he rifles through belongings to leave books and chocolates, and not, like Madame Beck, to take prints of keys. As Lucy tells us, "Never was a more undisguised schemer, a franker, looser, intriguer. He would analyse his own machinations: elaborately contrive plots, and forthwith indulge in explanatory boasts of their skill" (275). Finally, like others in the novel, Paul Emanuel is linked to that most unpleasant of enclosures, the confessional. But the lattice of Paul's confessional is "magic": unlike Père Silas, he uses his "post of observation" to seek understanding, and not to gain control.[18] Perched high above the garden of the Pensionnat, Paul has a perspective on life that is considerably loftier than that of anyone else in the novel—and certainly more elevated than Lucy's outlook.[19] When he is finally able to transcend the biases of his temperament and religious training, the "waspish little despot" reveals the singular wisdom of his viewpoint.

In a discussion of the unfortunate Zélie, Lucy outlines her own treatment by Paul Emanuel: "in some cases he had the terrible unerring penetration of instinct, and pierced in its hiding-place the last lurking thought of the heart ... " (306). What Paul Emanuel perceives in Lucy that no one else can see is the passion beneath the disguise, her yearning to be more than the looker-on she has declared herself to be. Paul's outburst at the Hôtel Crécy—described by Lucy as a satanic "hiss" from a "boa-constricter"—is revealing: "'vous avez l'air bien triste, soumise, rêveuse, mais vous ne l'êtes pas: c'est moi qui vous le dis: Sauvage! la flamme à l'âme, l'éclair aux yeux!'" (290). Recognizing the blazing soul beneath the cold and dark cloak of disguise, Paul delights in trampling on Lucy's dignity, goading and teasing her about her passive exterior. In so doing he evokes, somewhat as Vashti did, the carefully repressed passionate self beneath the disguise; he obliges Lucy to live rather than to look. Often described as a violent natural force—a clap of thunder, intemperate heat, a tiger, a gathering storm—Paul affects Lucy as powerfully as the elements do. He disturbs the subterranean complexities within her; he awakens both the strength of her spirit and the fear that attends this awakening.

Often Lucy delights in the novelty of Paul's treatment of her; at times she is pleased to emerge for him from the shadows. "'You are well habituated,'" she tells herself, "'to be passed by as a shadow in Life's sunshine: it is a new thing to see one testily lifting his hand to screen his eyes because you tease him with an obtrusive ray'" (304). Like her other Fate surrogates, Paul provides relief by addressing himself with decisiveness to Lucy's situation: "It seemed as if the presence of a nature so restless, chafing, thorny as that of M. Paul absorbed all feverish and unsettling influences like a magnet, and left me none but such as were placid and harmonious" (301). Only he arouses in Lucy the desire to tease, challenge, and vex; only with him can she summon enough distance on herself to find a sense of humour.

Yet Lucy's account of her developing esteem for Paul also betrays an unfortunate need to idealize. Described as her "Knight of Old," her "Christian hero," and especially her "master," Paul begins to resemble an idealized "personage" rather than that very real "salamander" he knows himself to be. It is not surprising that Lucy's devotion to Paul remains so disturbingly literary. For fundamentally her master represents a deep threat to Lucy. Shortly after they exchange their first confidences, for example, Lucy commits her "insane inconsistency" (351). Knowing that she is being sought by Paul, and anticipating, even desiring, a further confidence, she runs from him "on the wings of panic" (350). And later, she admits that the three years following Paul's departure "were the three happiest years of my life" (448). Lucy's reaction to Paul is not unlike Crimsworth's to Frances. When he steps out of the idealized autobiographical niche she has prepared for him into the blunt reality of intimacy, Lucy balks. She relishes the idea of a master, but avoids the reality of a lover.

77

Lucy Snowe's sexual repression, like Crimsworth's, plays an important role in her fears. The description of her first encounter with Paul suggestively uses sexual images to render her fear of visual penetration. Disturbed by his "sharp ring" from the "deep dell of dreamland" (117), Lucy feels that her peace has been violated: "The closed door of the first classe—my sanctuary —offered no obstacle; it burst open, and a paletôt and a bonnet grec filled the void; also two eyes first vaguely struck upon, and then hungrily dived into me" (118). And earlier we note the ambivalence about sexuality which Lucy betrays when she elaborately, yet cryptically, images a fellow teacher's profligacy:

> The Parisienne, on the other hand, was prodigal and profligate (in disposition, that is: as to action, I do not know). That latter quality showed its snake-head to me but once, peeping out very cautiously. A curious kind of reptile it seemed, judging from the glimpse I got; its novelty whetted my curiosity: if it would have come out boldly, perhaps I might philosophically have stood my ground, and coolly surveyed the long thing from forked tongue to scaly tail-tip; but it merely rustled in the leaves of a bad novel; and, on encountering a hasty and ill-advised demonstration of wrath, recoiled and vanished, hissing. She hated me from that day. (112)

It is not surprising that Lucy makes her home in a residence that formerly housed nuns. Dressed in her drab cloak and hood, she continually denies both her sexual and emotional nature.

There is, then, a peculiar appropriateness in the spectre which greets Lucy at the Pensionnat. Arriving in the "land of convents and confessionals" (87), she hears the legend of the nun who was buried alive "for some sin against her vow" (93). Dismissing the story as "romantic rubbish," Lucy proceeds to adopt the nun as a vehicle for conveying the moral purposes of her autobiography. The gusto with which she calls forth the nun—occasionally mistaking Madame Beck for an apparition, elaborately setting scenes for the ghost's arrival—is yet another of her many bold narrative manipulations. Lucy is, after all, aware as she writes her tale of the nun's real genesis; nevertheless, she takes care to exploit the figurative possibilities of the ghost to the fullest.

Lucy uses the figure of the nun to emphasize the distance between herself and the world in which she finds herself. A strident anti-Catholic, she sees in the nun an image of all that sets her apart from her society and, most important, from the man she finally loves. And the nun is also useful to Lucy as a cautionary example for herself. Early in the novel she claims to be in danger of forgetting, from time to time, that preordained niche that Fate has so deliberately carved for her in his universe. Occasionally she implies that Dr. John's attractiveness is too much for her to resist; she begins to hope that perhaps her Fate is not quite what she fears it will be. On such occasions Lucy conveniently parachutes in the nun to ward off her tendency to presumption. Thus, as she sits in the garret reading Dr. John's first letter, she describes the only moment of perfection she has yet experienced:

> This present moment had no pain, no blot, no want; full, pure, perfect, it deeply blessed me. A passing seraph seemed to have rested beside me, leaned towards my heart, and reposed on its throb a softening, cooling, healing, hallowing wing. (222)

The nun's first arrival, shattering her moment of repose, reminds Lucy of her folly. Lucy's nun, then, has two incarnations; as both an embodiment of Catholic tradition and a minatory puritan vision, it is a vehicle for the autobiographer's elucidation of her personal rationale.

What Lucy fails to see is the similarity between herself and her apparition. Buried alive in the garden for some unspecified but presumably sexual sin, the nun is amusingly juxtaposed by Brontë to Lucy herself. As an English Protestant schoolmistress, Lucy is also buried alive in the Pensionnat, and her deep sense of original sin never precludes sexual unease. Her adamant refusal to accept her own feelings for Dr. John is certainly nunnish (though without a religious dimension) in its dedication to chastity. Though Lucy interprets the nun's visits as warnings that her Reason should reassert itself over Feeling, the reader notes a premeditated refusal on her part to entertain any alternative possibilities to her life of lonely and celibate self-denial.

With each encounter of the apparition, Lucy feels that she is making progress on the road to self-knowledge. The reader, on the contrary, notes that with each visit Lucy becomes a bit more like her ghost. Though Dr. John promises "'To keep away the nun'" (231), his interest in Lucy—and, as important, hers in him—is not a sufficient antidote. After Lucy buries the letters which symbolize her feelings for Dr. John, she feels a new strength in the presence of the nun. In her eyes, an admirable leap into selfhood has been made; in the reader's eyes, however, Lucy has become almost as vestal as her former antagonist, the nun. And as the mystery of the nun is solved, we are left with a strong sense of the absurdity of the whole device. The image which imparted such resonance to an autobiographical quest has finally been only cloth and stuffing. As the figurative nun turns abruptly into a very literal practical joke, the serious pretensions of Lucy's narrative are ironically undercut. As Robert Keefe explains, "The use of this nun is ultimately highly ironic: far from representing a symbol of chastity sent from the world of death, the ghostly figure is in reality a young fop in search of a sex life."[20]

It is apparent that Lucy's concern about someone penetrating her disguise represents more than a fear of piercing eyes. To be seen through is to be understood; to be understood is to be mastered; and finally, though they are attractive to Lucy, masters constitute a deep threat to her shaky sexual nature. Paul Emanuel has plucked out the heart of Lucy's mystery, and, though she celebrates her commitment to him, we know that Madame Emanuel is not a role she could easily perform. Given the psychic needs of the narrator, Madame Emanuel is like Mrs. Rochester before the fire: she is simply implausible. We are not surprised to discover, then, in the last moments of the novel, that she will never be allowed to exist.

Toward the end of the novel, in a scene which presents her autobiography in microcosm, Lucy visits the park in Villette on the night of a fête. Significantly, she claims that the object of her visit—the thing she seeks with "the passionate thirst of unconscious fever"—is a basin of water in the park. The basin will be a mirror which will offer a reflection of herself and her world seen by the light of the moon:

> Amidst the glare, and hurry, and throng, and noise, I still secretly and chiefly longed to come on that circular mirror of crystal, and surprise the moon glassing therein her pearly front. (414)

Although Lucy claims to seek a mirror, however, it is clear by now that her autobiographical motives are considerably more complicated than she would allow. As we have seen, Lucy's view of how things must be is always stronger than her intimations of how things are; with Procrustean determination, she invariably stretches the body to suit the bed. Seeking a reflected image, she finds instead a means of making her own mirror; and calling herself a looker-on, she allows her eyes to rearrange what they perceive.

III.   Enclosure as Definition and Confinement

the garden was a trite, trodden-down place enough (94)

The need to contain experience by enclosing it—a need which we have seen to be characteristic of Brontë's earlier fictional autobiographers—dominates Lucy Snowe. Although she often complains about being enclosed by others (she refers to her "solitary confinement" in Madame Beck's Pensionnat and to the "hermit" position in which she finds herself when her friends forget her), she nevertheless reveals her own strong need to create enclosures throughout her story. Like William Crimsworth, Lucy deals with her students by enclosing them—both in closets and in disdainfully rigid formulae which she uses to explain their behaviour. Similarly, to cope with the Brettons' neglect, Lucy tries "different expedients to sustain and fill existence" (243). But all of her self-imposed regimens—elaborate lace-work, German, a "course of regular reading of the driest and thickest books in the library"—seek to remedy a constricted life by imposing even greater constrictions. And not unlike her "expedients" for circumscribing grief are her methods for handling joy. Upon receiving Dr. John's first letter, she triply encloses the treasure ("that treasure in the case, box, drawer upstairs" [220]) in order to enjoy it.

Lucy's enclosures, like Jane's and Crimsworth's, derive much of their ironic force from the double perspective which is implicit in them. In Lucy's eyes, enclosures are often a comforting source of self-definition. But to the reader, these same enclosures frequently point to a pronounced constriction of experience. What is defining for one appears as confining to another.

Like Jane and Crimsworth, Lucy presents her life as a moral mission.[21] She is aware in the beginning of a double challenge, a challenge both from herself and from her world. Lucy the orphan is convinced that she must embark on a journey toward self-knowledge. But self-knowledge is only half of her task. Crossing a figurative Styx into the city of Villette—a city in which she finds palaces indistinguishable from churches—Lucy, the innocent English Protestant, feels that she must also contend with a corrupt Catholic world. After only a short time in Villette she is called down by Fate from her watchtower of innocence (Madame Beck's nursery); she feels the pressure to survive in a decadent world without compromising her own integrity. The journey of her life that she maps out includes a number of developmental stages. Quickly Madame Beck's Pensionnat becomes a prison to her, and she portrays her symbolic death and rebirth into the Bretton home.[22] Yet this rebirth offers her no final solution (as her myth cautions her) because Graham is not a person to be paired with one of life's lookers-on. So Lucy effects her second death and rebirth, this time by burying her feelings (in the form of letters) for Graham. Now she is free to find the appropriate object of her love. The ghostly figure of the nun symbolizes for the autobiographer the obstacle which prevents a union with Paul Emanuel; as she becomes increasingly able to face the nun, she sees herself as triumphing over the Catholic conspiracy. In Lucy's scheme of things, the battle against self and society has been won. The final stage of Lucy's story, of course, comes with the loss of Paul Emanuel—a loss which represents that last and inevitable stroke of Lucy's implacable Fate.

Lucy's version of events imparts a pattern of forward motion to her life story. As she moves herself out of the nursery, out of the Pensionnat, and out of her professed delusions, she posits a view of herself as a dynamic, developing person. But Lucy's assertions of progress are countered at every turn by Brontë's assertions of stasis. Like Crimsworth, Lucy leaves her tower of innocence and joins the world of experience without increasing her awareness of either realm. And the enclosures she seeks as a means of ordering her experience become progressively imprisoning. For Brontë's narrators, nothing ever really changes—and the intractability of their situations is ironically emphasized by their own delusions of growth. The phrenological examination which Paul Emanuel makes of Lucy early in the novel is highly appropriate.[23] Predetermined cerebral bumps imply a view of character as something which does not change. Brontë's autobiographers fail even to embark on the journeys which they so carefully describe. At every point Brontë supplies the ironic counterpoint to Lucy's *Bildungsroman*.

As an alien in a hostile world, Lucy is strongly attracted by the seclusion and beauty of Madame Beck's garden: "where all is stone around, blank wall and hot pavement, how precious seems one shrub, how lovely an enclosed and planted spot of ground!" (93). As a newcomer to the Pensionnat, Lucy finds in the garden an escape from an oppressive world. Like William Crimsworth, she has a fixed notion of what her garden should do for her. Although she firmly disclaims the role of dreamer—"Suitor or admirer my very thoughts had not conceived" (97)—she cannot disguise her longings for a place of romance. Just after dismissing the legend of the nun as "romantic rubbish," she describes the garden, in spite of herself, in language which betrays these longings. She speaks of her desire to "keep tryst" with the moon, to "taste one kiss" of the breeze; she evokes trees which "nestled" and jasmine and ivy which "met and married" (93). But Lucy's desired Eden, like Crimsworth's, will not abide: "Presently the rude Real burst coarsely in—all evil, grovelling and repellent as she too often is" (97). The garden becomes the repository of everything unromantic in the novel, the centre of trivialization. De Hamal's casket speaks to Lucy of subversive love, and also informs her (as Crimsworth was informed) of others' very unflattering notions of herself. Dr. John's intrusions are decidedly sexual ("It was sacrilege. . . . He was lost in the shrubs, trampling flowers and breaking branches in his search—he penetrated at last the 'forbidden walk.'" [99]); they destroy the possibility of dreamy sanctuary for the vestal looker-on.

And as much spying goes on in the garden as anywhere else in the Pension-nat. The enclosure which Lucy seeks—in order to escape, to deal with her private passions, and to indulge in her romantic visions—turns out to be, like Crimsworth's, an obtrusively postlapsarian Eden. Lucy's complaint is predictable:

> My alley, and, indeed, all the walks and shrubs in the garden, had acquired a new, but not a pleasant interest; their seclusion was now become precarious; their calm insecure. That casement which rained billets had vulgarised the once dear nook it overlooked; and elsewhere, the eyes of the flowers had gained vision, and the knots in the tree-boles listened like secret ears. (102)

Her first attempt to create a sanctuary for herself in Villette has been thoroughly frustrating. Later in the novel, Lucy hopes she has replaced this artificial Eden with a real one. Yet she is never really at home in either. Both of Lucy's Edens partake stubbornly of the real world.

When, oppressed by the constricting world of the Pensionnat, Lucy is beset by acute hypochondria, she seeks solace in another enclosure. She flees to the confessional hoping for comfort from the chaos of her own frightening emotions. And at first she claims to have found it:

> the mere relief of communication in an ear which was human and sentient, yet consecrated—the mere pouring out of some portion of long accumulating, long pent-up pain into a vessel whence it could not be again diffused—had done me good. I was already solaced. (145)

But like her escape to the garden, this new strategy for a "prison break" also backfires.[24] The walls of the confessional become more confining than the walls of the dormitory. The comfort of the confessional, like that of other enclosures, is finally ironic. As Lucy discovers later, she has confessed to precisely the wrong man. Her association with Père Silas, initiated on the night of the confession, leads ultimately to the loss of Paul Emanuel. As the novel proceeds and the Catholic junta exercises its power, the confessional becomes a place of imprisonment and constriction. Even at its best—under the priestly eye and magic lattice of Paul Emanuel—the confessional merges with the garden; both become arenas for the observation of human foibles in their least attractive form. Again, as Lucy seeks safe enclosures, she manages to find only prisons.

The most extreme form of Lucy's need to enclose is her preoccupation with burial. Going beyond William Crimsworth, who spoke metaphorically of sealing his memories in urns, Lucy Snowe literally immures her past in the earth. In burying Dr. John's letters, she attempts to contain both her hope and her grief:

> "The Hope I am bemoaning suffered and made me suffer much: it did not die till it was full time; following an agony so lingering, death ought to be welcome." ... In the end I closed the eyes of my dead, covered its face, and composed its limbs with great calm. (267-68) ... I meant also to bury a grief. That grief over which I had lately been weeping, as I wrapped it in its winding-sheet, must be interred. (270)

For Lucy the scrupulous burial ritual is an episode of great importance; it is meant to mark a turning-point in her autobiography. In burying Dr. John's letters she sees herself as accepting a crucial lesson of her Fate. Her hopes for Dr. John (hopes which she has admitted only obliquely to the reader) have been, she is convinced, presumptuous. She must free herself from this darling of fortune in order to turn to a life better suited to a spectator. The burial represents to Lucy substantial progress in the direction of self-knowledge.

Lucy's emphatic enclosure, like William Crimsworth's, has been her morbid way of handling threateningly complicated feelings. Yet just as the nun in the adjoining grave was buried alive, so the tomb of Lucy's grief is not, we realize, really still. Even Lucy admits to occasional uneasiness about her farewell to Dr. John:

> Was this feeling dead? I do not know, but it was buried. Sometimes I thought the tomb unquiet, and dreamed strangely of disturbed earth, and of hair, still golden and living, obtruded through coffin-chinks. (329)

Her attempt to put Dr. John behind her never quite succeeds.

Immediately after burying the letters, Lucy discusses the "quality—electrical, perhaps—which acted in strange sort upon me. ... I felt, not happy, far otherwise, but strong with reinforced strength" (270). What Lucy perceives as a rebirth of new strength is actually a reinforced commitment to her personal myth. "If life be a war," she instructs herself to conclude, "it seemed my destiny to conduct it single-handed" (270). In burying the letters, Lucy has simply ratified the image of herself as looker-on. She can now refuse with new confidence the Homes' offer of a position as companion to Polly because, she says, she knows that her "vocation" (271) is elsewhere. The lesson which she feels she has learned gives her comfort: in burying her past, she feels reborn into her natural niche. Yet as she portrays herself rising from the grave of her disappointment, we see her digging herself into her preconceptions more deeply. More than ever, her cloak and hood resemble the conventual garments of the nun.

IV. The "Medium of Better Utterance":
Writing as Resurrection and Enclosure

a skeleton out of the dry bones of the real (365)

Unlike either of the earlier autobiographies, *Villette* calls deliberate attention to the written word. In *The Professor*, we recall, William Crimsworth wrote only one letter, which was an exercise in futility; aside from Hunsden's hasty notes, written correspondence did not figure prominently in the story. Jane Eyre received mostly business letters; though the news from Madeira certainly assisted in the story's denouement, the letters were not of much importance in themselves. In *Villette*, however, the letters that people write to one another are so important that they almost resemble discrete personages in Lucy's autobiographical drama. Lucy receives letters from Graham, Paul Emanuel, and Mrs. Bretton. Both Lucy and Polly devote much anxiety to drafting replies to the letters they receive. And palpable tension is often engendered by the long wait for a letter. Lucy approaches the post-hour "much as a ghost-seer might wait his spectre," fleeing to the garden and muffling her ears to avoid the "torturing clang" (246) of the postman's ring. Graham's letters, as we have seen, become the repository of considerable symbolic significance by means of Lucy's elaborate burial ritual. And Lucy's seven loneliest weeks she describes as being "as bare as seven sheets of blank paper" (242).

Lucy's obsession with letters betrays her discomfort with life. Time and again she reveals her preference for written rather than lived experience. Dr. John's unopened letter, described as an "untasted treasure," "all fair and inviolate" (217), is a purified version of a first sexual experience for Lucy; it is a virgin treasure that she can enjoy without the demands of mutuality. And later, when she loses the same letter in the attic, even the presence of Dr. John himself cannot console her. She prefers him in spiritualized form— embodied in his letter. When she says of the letter that she "prized it like the blood in my veins" (224), we are struck by her peculiar priority: the letter has become for her a living presence. For Lucy letters not only replace life, they also elevate life. They represent a transformation of what is unreliable, invading, and untidy—the presence of other people, that is—into what is manageable, unthreatening, and etherealized.

If Lucy finds solace in receiving letters, she also finds intense pleasure in writing them. In one of her characteristic dialogues with Reason—this time about the temptation of the pen—she is warned not to enjoy answering Graham's letters. She protests:

> "But I have talked to Graham, and you did not chide," I pleaded.
>
> "No," said she, "I needed not. Talk for you is good discipline. You converse imperfectly. While you speak, there can be no oblivion of inferiority—no encouragement to delusion: pain, privation, penury stamp your language"—
>
> "But," I again broke in, "where the bodily presence is weak and the speech contemptible, surely there cannot be error in making written language the medium of better utterance than faltering lips can achieve?"
>
> Reason only answered, "At your peril you cherish that idea, or suffer its influence to animate any writing of yours!" (207)

Lucy prefers writing to speaking because she is aware of the peculiar power of language. Through the "medium of better utterance" she can transform what is inferior, faltering, contemptible in herself into something animated. She can shape a better image of herself, fix a preferred persona. She can substitute for pain and penury something sustaining. As the beleaguered reader is well aware by now, Lucy is very much at home with language as a means both of self-defence and self-inflation. By verbalizing things, she hopes to make them so.

Even when she is not writing or receiving letters, Lucy's need for the written word is apparent. Her remarks about preparing an essay for Paul reveal that language relieves a felt need:

> ... I got books, read up the facts, laboriously constructed a skeleton out of the dry bones of the real, and then clothed them, and tried to breathe into them life, and in this last aim I had pleasure. (365)

For Lucy the written word not only promises to complete the self; it also promises to resurrect the self.[25] Faced with the dry bones of her experience, she writes, rather than lives, her life. Her autobiography mediates between herself and the world; it enables her to forge a reconstructed image.

Yet if writing brings comfort, it also—like the more physical enclosures in the novel—involves confinement. With Lucy Snowe as narrator, Charlotte Brontë posits the darkest view of art that she has yet suggested. For not only does Lucy, like Jane and Crimsworth, use her autobiography as a means of deceiving herself, but she also, as we have noted, uses its quite deliberately to deceive others. As Lucy encloses herself in her autobiography, then, Charlotte Brontë is again raising the spectre of art's ethical ambiguity.

Unlike the earlier novels, however, *Villette* provides an alternative to art as enclosure. Paul Emanuel, who, as we have noted, has the loftiest perspective in the novel, is also the consummate artist. Unlike Lucy and the others, Paul does not abuse the arts; his total engagement with life makes the false comforts which others seek from art unnecessary. Lucy directs the drama of her life with devious control, but of Paul we are told, "There was no sham and no cheat, and no hollow unreal in him" (449). In him, role and self are one. And Paul has no need to substitute letters for life; he tells her that "'My book is this garden; its contents are human nature...'" (331). But Paul's most important gift is something all the fictional autobiographers lack: he has, in abundance, the "impromptu faculty":

> He began to tell us a story. Well could he narrate: in such a diction as children love, and learned men emulate; a diction simple in its strength, and strong in its simplicity. There were beautiful touches in that little tale; sweet glimpses of feeling and hues of description that, while I listened, sunk into my mind, and since have never faded. He tinted a twilight scene —I hold it in memory still—such a picture I have never looked on from artist's pencil.
> I have said that, for myself, I had no impromptu faculty; and perhaps that very deficiency made me marvel the more at one who possessed it in perfection. M. Emanuel was not a man to write books; but I have heard him lavish, with careless, unconscious prodigality, such mental wealth as books seldom boast; his mind was indeed my library, and whenever it was opened to me, I entered bliss. (346)

Unlike Lucy Snowe, then, Paul Emanuel does not use art as a substitute for experience, nor does he use it to reconstruct his own image. Instead of reducing life, his art enriches it.

For Lucy Snowe, Emanuel supplies the living presence that his name suggests.[26] Although he is not "a man to write books," he sends letters to Lucy from Guadaloupe that differ from other letters in the novel in motive, style, and effect:

> By every vessel he wrote; he wrote as he gave and as he loved, in full-handed, full-hearted plenitude. He wrote because he liked to write; he did not abridge, because he cared not to abridge. He sat down, he took pen and paper, because he loved Lucy and had much to say to her; because he was faithful and thoughtful, because he was tender and true. There was no sham and no cheat, and no hollow unreal in him. Apology never dropped her slippery oil on his lips—never proffered, by his pen, her coward feints and paltry nullities: he would give neither a stone, nor an excuse—neither a scorpion, nor a disappointment; his letters were real food that nourished, living water that refreshed. (449)

Supplying from a distance what he provided by his presence—"real food that nourished, living water that refreshed"—Paul, until his death, makes the substitutions of art unnecessary for Lucy; his letters contain his "living presence." Once this living presence is removed, however, there is no longer anything to pull Lucy out of herself. Something must interpose itself between

Lucy and what is outside her; a mediator between her life and her world must be found.

Her autobiography becomes that mediator. But, as we have seen, the life that Lucy writes in lieu of Paul's living presence could not possibly be more unlike Emanuel than it is. Staged, contrived, self-protective, dishonest, distorted—the creation of Lucy's dark muse is an ironic monument indeed to a dead love. To the moment of Paul's death, Lucy continues her extraordinary manipulation. She pretends to hold out hope for a happy ending, yet at the reader who would wish for such an ending, she lashes out suddenly with a tone of bitter scorn. In Paul Emanuel's death at sea, his bereaved fiancée smugly recognizes the final stroke of a hostile Fate—part of her preordained personal mythology. In her eyes, the thesis about herself that she set out to prove has been victoriously demonstrated. Deprived of her Emanuel, she turns to her pen in order to resurrect herself. But in our eyes her resurrection is ultimately an interment.

CHAPTER FIVE

Strait and Secret Minds

Life I must bound, existence sum
In the strait limits of one mind;
That mind my own. Oh! narrow cell . . .

CHARLOTTE BRONTË[1]

To "sum" an existence, "bound" a life, and find safety in the "strait limits" of an enclosed mind—this is the compelling motive of Charlotte Brontë's fictional autobiographers. All three autobiographers have in common their need to interpret reductively both their own natures and the worlds in which they live. Repressing what their more instinctual impulses tell them about the complex truths of experience, they all generate personal mythologies by which to rationalize their lives. Their mythologies present the life story as a pattern of progress—a paradigm for the growth of insight, the development of character, and the fulfillment of personal destiny.

In each of the three situations, however, the novel itself answers its narrator by raising questions which implicitly but decisively undercut the auto-biographer's self-portrait. As Lucy Snowe engineers her own rebirth, the reader senses that he is attending at a burial. The art gallery of William Crimsworth's past dissolves into a narrow cell. And Jane Eyre's effusions of bliss sound disturbingly like cries of despair. What emerges from these auto-biographies, then, is Brontë's deep skepticism about the adequacy of her narrators' constructs. Brontë the creator knew that art which evades the ambiguities of experience only abuses both itself and the life it attempts to render. And she demurred implicitly from her narrators' assumption (an assumption shared by many of her own contemporaries) that life is most faithfully rendered through paradigms of progress and moral growth.

Given that Brontë deeply distrusted the fabrication of patterns of growth and fulfillment, we must be wary of characterizing her own career in neat evolutionary terms. To address her artistry as though it were progressing toward a fixed point of achievement is to impose a pattern on the works; and, more important, this approach denies the novels their rich variety. Though three of Brontë's four novels employ a similar kind of narrative strategy, it is the striking differences among the works, rather than their underlying similarities, which leave the greatest impression. In each of her fictional autobiographies, Brontë was setting new problems for herself, meeting different challenges. Nevertheless, the novels can be considered as a group—and even as a group which moves in a certain direction. As Brontë's narrators become more aware of themselves as artists, they learn to employ more competently—and more questionably—the resources of their craft. (Consequently, they place greater demands on the reader, who must exercise increasing vigilance in his response to their autobiographical constructs.) Taken together, the fictional autobiographers adumbrate a progressively darkening view of the artist's presentation of himself. The movement from William Crimsworth through Jane Eyre to Lucy Snowe is a movement from blindness to self-delusion to the deliberate delusion of others.

William Crimsworth is an aesthete by avocation. Using his active imagination misanthropically, to schematize his world, he seals himself hermetically within his own "strait and secret nook." As he glibly turns his very ambiguous life into a moralistic success story, he remains oblivious to the deeper truths which undercut his victory. His attitude toward the reader of his autobiography is similar to his attitude toward the world: gratified by his title of "Professor," he addresses both with supercilious complacency. He needs, and expects, an audience which will receive passively the lessons of his hard-earned wisdom. The reader, however, recognizing Crimsworth's complete self-absorption, is not tempted (nor, indeed, invited) to ratify at any point the autobiographer's view of things. Instead, we find ourselves just outside the narrow cell of this professedly virtuous mind. Through our experience of Crimsworth's disconcerting autobiography, we come to realize how high-mindedness is able not only to coexist with, but even to nourish, callous insensitivity.

Jane Eyre is more conscious than Crimsworth of her role as artist, and her artistic gift is more substantial. She is a self-professed maker of images, both on canvas and on the printed page. Dominated by a romantic imagination, she renders her story in a manner which is more compelling than Crimsworth's. Indeed, at many points in her autobiography she both asks for and earns our ungrudging assent as we participate in her quest for identity. But the sympathy we feel for Jane is precisely what constitutes the novel's greatest challenge. For insofar as we identify with her struggles, we may fail to recognize the inadequacy of the interpretation she imposes on her unfolding life. The reader's need for wish-fulfillment, in other words, is likely in this novel to become tangled with the narrator's. Ultimately, it is her artistic sensibility which tempts both Jane and her reader to avoid the "severe Truth"; her efforts to seek the truth give way to the bright visions of her imagination. As she transforms her life into a fairy-tale and her autobiography into a novel, we recognize her pronounced tendency to self-delusion.

Jane Eyre's self-delusion, however, does not rival Lucy Snowe's blatant dishonesties. The most audacious artist of the three, Lucy uses her gift—a brilliant facility with the power of language—to delude others. Lucy enters her autobiography determined to forestall self-knowledge; with cynical fatalism, she has decided not even to search for that elusive truth which evades Crimsworth and defeats Jane. But more disturbing than Lucy's self-delusion is her tendency to delude others. A "looker-on at life," she virtually transforms herself in her autobiography into a pair of voyeuristic eyes which glance both toward and away from herself. Coldly and scornfully she manipulates both her associates and her reader into collusion with her myth. Lucy's eyes are very much on her reader—but she neither appeals to her audience, as Jane does, nor presupposes its assent, as Crimsworth does. Instead, like everything in Lucy's world (including even her own self-portrait) we become a pawn to be controlled by the determined autobiographer. Lucy's motives for writing are incomprehensible, her reasons for distortion baffling. She seems to represent the artistic impulse in its most unpleasant incarnation. It is with the art of Lucy Snowe, then, that Brontë raises the bleakest questions about the morality of the creative gift.

When Brontë described her own artistic credo, she did so in metaphors of religious worship:

> The first duty of an author is, I conceive, a faithful allegiance to Truth and Nature; his second, such a conscientious study of Art as shall enable him to interpret eloquently and effectively the oracles delivered by those two great deities.[2]

William Crimsworth, Jane Eyre, and Lucy Snowe invert the hierarchy of this commitment; in their self-portraits, Truth and Nature become servile handmaidens to Art. To extend Brontë's own metaphor, the art of the fictional autobiographers is not worship, but idolatry; the narrators bear devotion to a lesser deity. Yet, ironically, it is by means of the artful distortions of these fictional creators that Brontë herself was able to render allegiance to her own deities—to create a truth-telling art. We begin to sense Brontë's pervasive but quiet presence in her novels only after we have penetrated the masks of three far less accomplished artists.

NOTES

CHAPTER ONE: The Cover of the Mask

[1] Quoted in Elizabeth Gaskell, *The Life of Charlotte Brontë*, ed. Alan Shelston (Harmondsworth, England: Penguin, 1975), p. 94.

[2] "Charlotte Brontë," in *Hours in a Library*, rev. ed. (London: Smith, Elder, 1892), III, 6-7. Even in this extreme form, the biographical approach to Brontë persisted for many years. Published as late as 1934, David Cecil's opinions are similar to Stephen's. See *Early Victorian Novelists: Essays in Revaluation* (London: Constable, 1934), pp. 109-44.

[3] Robert Martin, *The Accents of Persuasion* (London: Faber and Faber, 1966), p. 18.

[4] Earl A. Knies, for instance, writes an introductory chapter warning against improper autobiographical inferences but later invokes Brontë's life to explain supposed faults in *The Professor. The Art of Charlotte Brontë* (Athens: Ohio Univ. Press, 1969), pp. 94-96.

[5] Helene Moglen interprets the life and work in "psychosexual" terms with an emphasis on the tension in Brontë between the lure of regressive sexual fantasies and the desire to assert an autonomous self. *Charlotte Brontë: The Self Conceived* (New York: Norton, 1976). For Robert Keefe, the guilt engendered by the early death of her mother is the key to Brontë's personality and art. *Charlotte Brontë's World of Death* (Austin: Univ. of Texas Press, 1979). The chapters on Brontë by Sandra M. Gilbert and Susan Gubar (*The Madwoman in the Attic: The Woman Writer and the Nineteenth-Century Literary Imagination* [New Haven: Yale Univ. Press, 1979]) cannot properly be called psychobiography. These critics locate the essential stimulus of Brontë's art not so much in her individual history (biographical or psychological) as in the literary determinations of her gender. What all three studies have in common is their emphasis on the involuntary nature of Brontë's writing.

[6] Even some of the best modern critical studies occasionally attempt to impose on the texts of the novels hypothetical constructions of Brontë's opinions. See, for example, Kate Millett, *Sexual Politics* (New York: Avon, 1969), pp. 201-02; Martin, p. 166; Terry Eagleton, *Myths of Power: A Marxist Study of the Brontës* (London: Macmillan, 1975), pp. 11-13; and Tom Winnifrith, *The Brontës* (New York: Collier, 1977), p. 123.

[7] F. T. C. Flahiff, "Formative Ideas in the Novels of Charlotte and Emily Brontë," Diss. University of Toronto 1965, p. 7.

[8] Quoted in Alan Shelston's Introduction to Mrs. Gaskell's *Life*, p. 26.

[9] Alan Shelston's divided response testifies to the persuasiveness of the portrait. Although he analyzes keenly the partialities of Mrs. Gaskell's biography, he concludes his Introduction by stressing "the overall truth of her presentation . . ." (p. 36).

[10] See Tom Winnifrith's discussion of the vicissitudes of the Brontë letters in *The Brontës and Their Background* (New York: Barnes and Noble, 1973).

[11] See *The Brontës: Their Lives, Friendships & Correspondence in Four Volumes* (Oxford: Shakespeare Head Press, 1932), II, 255. (Hereafter these volumes will be cited at *LFC*.) See also Mrs. Gaskell, p. 350. Anne and Charlotte used the pseudonym of "Brown" on the occasion of their first visit to London, when no one knew even their "Brontë" identity.

[12] The three were her father, her brother Branwell, and Ellen Nussey. See Mrs. Gaskell, pp. 318-19 and Clement Shorter, *The Brontës: Life and Letters* (New York: Haskell House, 1969), I, 452.

[13] See *LFC*, II: 211, 227-28.

[14] *LFC*, II, 174.

[15] *LFC*, IV, 13.

[16] *LFC*, II, 3.

[17] *LFC*, III, 218.

[18] For other examples, see *LFC*, III: 38, 50, 324.

[19] *LFC*, III, 15.

[20] Flahiff, p. 7. See also Knies, p. 59, for a discussion of the pseudonym as a technique for providing distance.

[21] Quoted in Leon Edel, *Literary Biography* (Toronto: Univ. of Toronto Press, 1957), p. 45.

[22] "The Lesson of Balzac," in *The Future of the Novel: Essays on the Art of Fiction*, ed. Leon Edel (New York: Vintage Books, 1956), p. 101.

[23] Earl A. Knies makes this comment (p. 37) as he concludes his chapter called "Art and Autobiography," in which he demonstrates persuasively that the biographical approach is untenable.

[24] *LFC*, III, 322.

[25] For nineteenth-century attitudes toward autobiography, see Keith Rinehart, "The Victorian Approach to Autobiography," *Modern Philology*, 51 (1954), 177-86; Wayne Shumaker, *English Autobiography: Its Emergence, Materials, and Form* (Berkeley: Univ. of California Press, 1954); and Richard D. Altick, *Lives and Letters: A History of Literary Biography in England and America* (New York: Knopf, 1965), p. 104.

[26] For some references to autobiographies that Brontë was reading, see *LFC*, III: 88, 98, 150, 174, 210.

27 See Lawrence Jay Dessner's comments on "Charlotte Brontë's enduring interest in narrative techniques, in the separation and characterization of the narrator, in, in short, the potential uses of the controlled point of view." *The Homely Web of Truth: A Study of Charlotte Brontë's Novels* (The Hague: Mouton, 1975), p. 7 et passim.

28 Janice Carlisle, "The Face in the Mirror: *Villette* and the Conventions of Autobiography," *ELH*, 46 (1979), 266. Carlisle's study came to my attention after my manuscript had been completed. Although her examination of autobiographical conventions in *Villette* yields perceptions which are at some points encouragingly similar to mine, our approaches differ substantially. She interprets the novel's autobiographical form in terms of the "problematic function" of memory and emphasizes Lucy Snowe's dependence "on essentially subversive ways of appeasing memory" (p. 265). In my view, the issues raised by the narrator's self-representation in *Villette* (and indeed in the other first-person narratives) are more disquieting.

29 See, for instance, Leslie Stephen's characterization of autobiography as "the man's own shadow cast upon the coloured and distorting mists of memory" in his essay "Autobiography." *Hours in a Library*, rev. ed. (London: Smith, Elder, 1892), III, 237. For a fuller, more recent discussion of autobiographical truth, see Roy Pascal, *Design and Truth in Autobiography* (London: Routledge and Kegan Paul, 1960).

30 *Aspects of Biography* (New York: Frederick Ungar, 1929), pp. 157-58.

31 See "The Personal Myth: A Problem in Psychoanalytic Technique," *Journal of the American Psychoanalytic Association*, 4, No. 4 (1956), 653-81. See also Erik Homburger Erikson, "The Problem of Ego Identity," *Journal of the American Psychoanalytic Association*, 4, No. 1 (1956), 56-121.

32 Kris, p. 679.

33 Kris, p. 678.

34 *LFC*, I, 163.

35 For a discussion of Foster's essay, see Rinehart, 178-80.

36 Rinehart, 179.

37 Margaret Anne Halloran discusses *The Professor* and *The Pilgrim's Progress* in "The Apocalypse of Charlotte Brontë," an unpublished paper.

38 The term is Henry James's, quoted in Patrick Cruttwell, "Makers and Persons," *Hudson Review*, 12 (1959-60), 493.

39 Frederick R. Karl, in "The Brontës: The Self Defined, Redefined, and Refined" briefly discusses enclosure as both a refuge and a snare. Unfortunately, Karl is so concerned with larger issues that his readings of the novels are not fully elaborated. See *The Victorian Experience: The Novelists*, ed. Richard A. Levine (Athens: Ohio Univ. Press, 1976).

40 Knies' attempt to distance the novels from Brontë's life brings him to the misleading position that "Another highly important aspect of Charlotte's

life is totally absent in those of her heroines: her art. None of them meets aristocrats and literary figures; none has the pleasure or pain of reading a review of her new novel" (pp. 37-38). But the narrators' engagement in the creation of their own autobiographies qualifies them as practising artists. And, as my discussion of the works emphasizes, they become increasingly aware of themselves as artists.

41 The term is Shumaker's, p. 106.

42 For some other references to biographies in *LFC*, see I: 122, 159; II: 222; III: 20, 155, 268.

43 See Altick, p. 77.

44 John A. Garraty, *The Nature of Biography* (London: Jonathan Cape, 1957), p. 91. See also Harold Nicolson's discussion of the strain of "hagiography" as an obstacle to the tradition of biography epitomized by Boswell. *The Development of English Biography* (London: The Hogarth Press, 1927).

45 Quoted in Garraty, p. 93.

46 Quoted in Garraty, p. 94. Carlyle made this famous remark when Sir Walter Scott's biographer, Lockhart, was attacked for his cautious criticisms.

47 *LFC*, II, 225.

48 See especially Brontë's comments on Southey and Dr. Arnold. *LFC*, III: 98, 178.

49 *LFC*, III, 322.

50 See also references in *LFC*, II: 255 and 319.

51 *LFC*, II, 243.

52 See Knies, Chapter 2.

53 *LFC*, IV, 76-77.

54 Brontë is referring in this instance to unfavourable reviews. *LFC*, IV, 50.

CHAPTER TWO: *The Professor*

1 See Winnifrith, p. 88.

2 Quoted in Mrs. Gaskell, p. 305.

3 *LFC*, II, 161.

4 Winnifrith, p. 101.

5 W. A. Craik, *The Brontë Novels* (London: Methuen, 1968), p. 48.

6 Martin, p. 34.

7 Martin, p. 41.

8 See, for example, the chapters on the novel in Winnifrith and Dessner.

⁹ See Margaret Blom, *Charlotte Brontë*, Twayne's English Authors Series (Boston: G. K. Hall, 1977), p. 79.

¹⁰ Winifred Gérin advances this argument quite explicitly. See *Charlotte Brontë: The Evolution of Genius* (Oxford: Clarendon, 1967), pp. 316-32.

¹¹ Quoted in Pascal, *Design and Truth in Autobiography*, p. 62.

¹² Winnifrith, p. 90.

¹³ Charlotte Brontë, *The Professor*, ed. Phyllis Bentley (London: Collins, 1954), p. 299; hereafter cited in the text.

¹⁴ See *LFC*, II, 161, for Brontë's comments to W. S. Williams about illustrating her novels: "... I hope no one will be at the trouble to make portraits of my characters." Considering the intentional ambiguities in Brontë's conception of her characters, it is fortunate that drawings were not done; visual images would necessarily have oversimplified the characters. Smith, Elder and Co. honoured Brontë's wishes in their 1875 edition of the *Life and Works of Charlotte Brontë and her Sisters*: they illustrated only landscapes and houses.

¹⁵ The notion of memories sealed in urns has at least two notable historical precedents which may have implications for Brontë's use. Sir Thomas Browne, in his "Urne-Buriall" ("Hydriotaphia," in *Sir Thomas Browne: The Major Works*, ed. C. A. Patrides [Harmondsworth, England: Penguin, 1977], pp. 261-315), emphasized the vanity of earthly memorials and the futility of man's hopes for immortality by means of these memorials. And John Locke, in his *An Essay Concerning Human Understanding* (ed. Raymond Wilburn [London: Dent, 1947]), discussed, using the same image, the fallibility of memory: "Thus the ideas, as well as children, of our youth, often die before us: and our minds represent to us those tombs to which we are approaching; where, though the brass and marble remain, yet the inscriptions are effaced by time, and the imagery moulders away" (p. 56). Brontë's self-deluded autobiographers, all of whom bury and hope to resurrect their pasts, partake of both the vanity which Browne deplores and the faulty recollection of the past which Locke attributes to all men.

¹⁶ Robert Martin sees the absence of further reference to the fourth picture as a flaw in the novel: "The author's red herrings succeed only in calling unproductive attention to herself and in distracting the reader from his involvement in the novel" (p. 38).

¹⁷ Lawrence Dessner discusses Crimsworth's psychosexual impulses as they are manifested in a number of his relationships (pp. 49-63).

¹⁸ Cynthia A. Linder, in her *Romantic Imagery in the Novels of Charlotte Brontë* (London: Macmillan, 1978), discusses Crimsworth's movement from Reuter's artificial garden to Daisy Lane's natural one (pp. 25ff.). In my opinion, Linder's discussion of this image and others neglects the novels' ironies. As I attempt to demonstrate, there are often discrepancies between the autobiographers' figurative purposes and the author's.

¹⁹ F. T. Flahiff has suggested that the several references in the novel to

things that are green (such as the doormat by Frances' flat and her carpet) allude to her possible promiscuity.

20 *Their Proper Sphere: A Study of the Brontë Sisters as Early-Victorian Female Novelists* (London: Edward Arnold, 1966), p. 200.

21 Martin, p. 40.

22 Ewbank, p. 188.

23 Pascal, *Design and Truth in Autobiography*, pp. 189-90.

24 See Linder's discussion of nature imagery in the novel (pp. 29ff.).

25 Charlotte Brontë, *Five Novelettes: Passing Events, Julia, Mina Laury, Captain Henry Hastings, Caroline Vernon*, ed. Winifred Gérin (London: The Folio Press, 1971).

26 *LFC*, II, 136.

27 For example, Tom Winnifrith, whose position on the question of Crimsworth's development is more cautious than most, argues that "Crimsworth is a pitiful creature at the beginning of the novel and is perhaps unduly complacent at the end, but at any rate, *The Professor* traces some pattern of spiritual growth" (p. 96). Elsewhere (p. 51) Winnifrith notes that the Crimsworth of Daisy Lane is much changed from his former self.

CHAPTER THREE: *Jane Eyre*

1 Quoted in Mrs. Gaskell, p. 305.

2 See Gérin, p. 337.

3 From Brontë's preface to *The Professor*, written after the publication of *Shirley*. Quoted in *The Professor*, ed. Bentley, p. 163.

4 Martin, p. 108.

5 In the opinion of Cynthia A. Linder, Brontë's use of fictional autobiography places the novels within the Romantic tradition: "The autobiographical form that Brontë has used, suggesting that it will present a subjective point of view, sets the novel in the Romantic tradition of writing, as it is the essence of Romantic philosophies that man only regards, and singles out for special comment, those aspects of life which are of importance to himself . . ." (31). This argument fails to emphasize that the novels are not Brontë's autobiographies. Although the autobiography that Jane Eyre writes may be in the Romantic tradition, the novel that Charlotte Brontë writes is not; and although Jane Eyre may be a fine example of a Romantic sensibility, her creator is not.

6 Quoted in *The Brontës: The Critical Heritage*, ed. Miriam Allott (London: Routledge and Kegan Paul, 1974), p. 303.

7 Quoted in Gérin, p. 477.

8 Dessner, p. 73.

9 *LFC*, II, 151.

¹⁰ Charlotte Brontë, *Jane Eyre*, ed. Jane Jack and Margaret Smith (Oxford: Clarendon, 1969), p. 4; hereafter cited in the text.

¹¹ Like Crimsworth, Jane sometimes uses images of enclosure to characterize both her own situation and that of others. These images are less complicated than the unlocked room by which Brontë portrays Jane to the reader; they carry more conventional associations. Jane indicates her frustrations at Lowood, for example, by describing its garden: "The garden was a wide enclosure, surrounded with walls so high as to exclude every glimpse of prospect..." (54). Similarly, Jane's houses become prisons to her when she feels the need for a change. And she neatly confines Eliza and Georgiana Reed into a constricted existence by means of enclosure images: "... I beheld one the cynosure of a ball-room, the other the inmate of a convent cell..." (304). Like Crimsworth's framed pictures, these enclosures reveal an attempt to schematize the world.

¹² See Chapter One, pp. 20-21.

¹³ See, for example, Jane Millgate, "Narrative Distance in *Jane Eyre*: The Relevance of the Pictures," *Modern Language Review*, 63 (1968), 315-19; Barbara Gates, "'Visionary Woe' and Its Revision: Another Look at Jane Eyre's Pictures," *Ariel*, 7, No. 4 (1976), 36-49; Thomas Langford, "The Three Pictures in *Jane Eyre*," *Victorian Newsletter*, No. 31 (1967), pp. 47-48; and Lawrence E. Moser, S.J., "From Portrait to Person: A Note on the Surrealistic in *Jane Eyre*," *Nineteenth-Century Fiction*, 20 (1965-66), 275-81.

¹⁴ The irony of Jane's solution is figured by an enclosure image which ends the scene: "Feverish with vain labour, I got up and took a turn in the room; undrew the curtain, noted a star or two, shivered with cold, and again crept to bed" (102). In her need to look beyond her small room at "a star or two," but also to creep to her bed, we note Jane's characteristic ambivalence. It is this same ambivalence which creates in Jane the need for formulae (like "a new servitude") by which she attempts to solve her inner conflicts.

¹⁵ This quotation, not referred to elsewhere in the chapter, is from Jane's description of the women at the house party: "all had a sweeping amplitude of array that seemed to magnify their persons as a mist magnifies the moon" (214).

¹⁶ Millgate, p. 317.

¹⁷ See Robert Keefe, *Charlotte Brontë's World of Death* (Austin, Univ. of Texas Press, 1979), p. 108, where he refers to Brocklehurst as "a combination of the devil and Red Riding Hood's wolf."

¹⁸ Jane's own need to create dichotomies by which to explain herself has tempted many critics to find the novel's organizing principles in the nature/grace or duty/passion distinctions. These readings assume that there is little distance between Jane and Brontë.

¹⁹ See Robert B. Heilman, "Charlotte Brontë, Reason, and the Moon," *Nineteenth-Century Fiction*, 14 (1959-60), 283-302, for an interesting account

of the many and complicated appearances of this image in the novels. Heilman's conclusions differ from mine; he sees the moon images as direct expressions of Brontë's positions, and thus he does not find that these images are ironic.

20 Millgate, p. 318.

21 The general approach of these critics to *Jane Eyre* is to formulate its significance in moral and religious terms. See, for example, Martin: *"Jane Eyre* is at bottom . . . largely a religious novel, concerned with the meaning of religion to man and its relevance to his behaviour" (p. 81); Dessner: "It is the moral and religious import of human passion and sexuality that is examined in *Jane Eyre,* and we forget this at the risk of misreading" (p. 72); and Winnifrith: *". . . Jane Eyre* can and should be seen as a deeply satisfying statement of one person's solution to the problem of keeping a proper balance between altruism and selfishness" (p. 123).

22 Martin, p. 83.

23 "'All Passion Spent': A Revaluation of *Jane Eyre,*" *University of Toronto Quarterly,* 19 (1949-50), 124.

24 Edgar F. Shannon, Jr., "The Present Tense in *Jane Eyre,*" *Nineteenth-Century Fiction,* 10 (1955-56), 145.

25 Winnifrith, pp. 109, 119.

26 Martin, pp. 90-91, 96-97.

27 Miltonic allusions are numerous in the novels, and Brontë's treatment of them is very complicated; the subject deserves extensive investigation.

28 W. A. Craik's suggestion that the reader assumes the Rochesters will leave Ferndean is, in my opinion, unfounded. See Craik, p. 113.

29 See Ewbank, p. 184.

CHAPTER FOUR: *Villette*

1 Charlotte Brontë, *Villette* (London: Dent, 1957), p. 36; hereafter cited in the text.

2 See, for example, Jean Frantz Blackall, "Point of View in *Villette,*" *Journal of Narrative Technique,* 6 (1977), 14-28; Earl A. Knies, *The Art of Charlotte Brontë,* Chapter 6; Robert A. Colby, *"Villette* and the Life of the Mind," *PMLA,* 75 (1960), 410-19; and, more recently, Janice Carlisle, "The Face in the Mirror: *Villette* and the Conventions of Autobiography."

3 See Knies, p. 184: "The problem of identity is important in all of Charlotte Brontë's works, but in the ambiguous world of *Villette,* it becomes the central question."

4 Blackall, p. 16.

5 *Early Victorian Novelists: Essays in Revaluation,* p. 117.

6 For the account of Vashti (wife of King Ahasuerus), who refused to obey

her inebriated husband's order to come to his banquet-hall to show her beauty to the guests, see Esther I:10,19.

[7] Robert Keefe, commenting on the scene in which Lucy faints after confessing, suggests that for Lucy "existence itself is a prison, the body its walls, and eternity has become the real home." See *Charlotte Brontë's World of Death*, p. 169.

[8] Brontë explored the notion of confounded language most fully in *Shirley*.

[9] Many critics have also mentioned the place names in *Villette*. See, for instance, Martin, pp. 154ff. See also Georgia Dunbar, "Proper Names in *Villette*," *Nineteenth-Century Fiction*, 15 (1960), 77-80.

[10] Frederick R. Karl, in "The Brontës: The Self Defined, Redefined, and Refined," places the Brontës within what he calls the "literature of enclosure" tradition, and comments on the simultaneity of enclosure and observation (or voyeurism). See *The Victorian Experience: The Novelists*, pp. 121-50.

[11] See Chapter Three, n. 13 and n. 16, for reference to the Millgate quotation.

[12] *Myths of Power: A Marxist Study of the Brontës*, p. 63.

[13] Eagleton, p. 63.

[14] In a discussion of Lucy's many "*alter egos*," Jean Frantz Blackall touches on several of the details which I cite in this paragraph. Blackall's emphasis, however, is different from mine; she suggests that the *alter egos* are "at once elucidating aspects of Lucy's character and desire and providing human encounters that precipitate her into self-revealing behavior." See Blackall, pp. 16-21.

[15] See Blackall, p. 21: "Despite her disclaimer of similar 'gifts,' Lucy strikingly resembles Mme. Beck, who is her counterpart in certain traits, and whose ultimate fate resembles Lucy's own." See also Eagleton, pp. 65-66: "Madame Beck is at once her oppressor and an image of the icy rational power she herself wants to possess."

[16] *Their Proper Sphere: A Study of the Brontë Sisters as Early-Victorian Female Novelists*, p. 176.

[17] Differences of opinion among critics about Paul Emanuel are pronounced. An example of a less sympathetic reading is that of Frederick Karl: "His reliance on his manhood is virtually pathological in its implications, for his defense of masculinity is attached to several other aspects of his character: his stance as Bonaparte; his constant voyeurism—beyond the call of an inquisitive schoolmaster; his need to keep others dependent upon him—disguised as charity . . ." (p. 130).

[18] I am indebted to F. T. Flahiff for his remarks about perspective in the novel. For his description of the city of Villette as a labyrinth, see his "Formative Ideas in the Novels of Charlotte and Emily Brontë," p. 169.

[19] In *Villette* it is Paul Emanuel who has a post of observation overlooking the garden. In *The Professor* it was William Crimsworth who occupied this position, although ironically his view was obstructed by a boarded window and he certainly did not learn anything by means of his elevated vantage point. The closest Lucy comes to such a vantage point is during her brief term of service in Madame Beck's nursery; although as governess she remains above the fray of the Pensionnat, she never looks down from her elevated position on the proceedings below.

[20] Keefe, p. 181.

[21] See Keefe, p. 161, for a discussion of Lucy's mission as an exile.

[22] When he cites Maud Bodkin's rebirth archetype as a structural device in the novel, Earl A. Knies fails to emphasize the ironies inherent in Lucy's rebirths. See Knies, p. 198.

[23] For comments on the implications of Brontë's use of phrenology and physiognomy, see Andrew D. Hook, "Charlotte Brontë, the Imagination, and *Villette*," in *The Brontës: A Collection of Critical Essays*, ed. Ian Gregor (Englewood Cliffs, New Jersey: Prentice-Hall, 1970), p. 149, n. 9, and Robert A. Colby, p. 415.

[24] See Millett, *Sexual Politics*, p. 200: "Escape is all over the book; *Villette* reads like one long meditation on a prison break."

[25] All autobiographers re-create the self, but Brontë's autobiographers seem to need to resurrect the self. In *Villette*, of the three novels, the notion is most explicit and most fully explored. See Keefe, p. 171, for comments on writing as consolation and resurrection.

[26] Literally, "God with us." A number of critics have mentioned also the significance of Emanuel as Deliverer. Although my reading emphasizes another facet of the name, both allusions are pertinent. Even as Lucy's Deliverer, however, the thrust of Paul Emanuel's name is ironic; the potential saviour is lost at sea.

CHAPTER FIVE: Strait and Secret Minds

[1] From "Reason," quoted by Gérin, pp. 279ff. These lines did not appear in the final version of the poem, which was entitled "Frances."

[2] *LFC*, II, 243.

BIBLIOGRAPHY

Primary Sources

Brontë, Charlotte. *Five Novelettes: Passing Events, Julia, Mina Laury, Captain Henry Hastings, Caroline Vernon.* Ed. Winifred Gérin. London: The Folio Press, 1971.

——. *Jane Eyre.* Ed. Jane Jack and Margaret Smith. Oxford: Clarendon, 1969.

——. *The Professor, Tales From Angria, Emma: A Fragment.* Ed. Phyllis Bentley. London: Collins, 1954.

——. *Shirley.* Ed. Andrew and Judith Hook. Harmondsworth, England: Penguin, 1974.

——. *Villette.* Introd. Margaret Lane. Everyman's Library. London: Dent, 1957.

The Brontës: Their Lives, Friendships and Correspondence. Ed. T. J. Wise and J. A. Symington. Shakespeare Head Brontë. 4 vols. Oxford: Shakespeare Head Press, 1932.

Shorter, Clement. *The Brontës: Life and Letters.* 2 vols. London: Hodder and Stoughton, 1908. rpt. New York: Haskell House, 1969.

Secondary Sources

Allott, Miriam, ed. *The Brontës: The Critical Heritage.* London: Routledge and Kegan Paul, 1974.

——, ed. *"Jane Eyre" and "Villette": A Casebook.* London: Macmillan, 1973.

Altick, Richard D. *Lives and Letters: A History of Literary Biography in England and America.* New York: Knopf, 1965.

Björk, Harriet. *The Language of Truth: Charlotte Brontë, The Woman Question, and the Novel.* Lund: Gleerup, 1974.

Blackall, Jean Frantz. "Point of View in *Villette.*" *Journal of Narrative Technique,* 6 (1977), 14-28.

Blom, Margaret Howard. *Charlotte Brontë.* Twayne's English Authors Series. Boston: G. K. Hall, 1977.

Bonnycastle, S. R. "The Construction of the Self in Four Romantic Autobiographies." Diss. Univ. of Kent at Canterbury, 1976.

Booth, Wayne C. *The Rhetoric of Fiction.* Chicago: Univ. of Chicago Press, 1961.

Browne, Sir Thomas. "Hydriotaphia." In *Sir Thomas Browne: The Major Works.* Ed. C. A. Patrides. Harmondsworth, England: Penguin, 1977, pp. 261-315.

Bunyan, John. *The Pilgrim's Progress.* Ed. James Blanton Wharey. 2nd ed. Rev. by Roger Sharrock. Oxford: Clarendon, 1960.

Burkhart, Charles. "Another Key Word for *Jane Eyre.*" *Nineteenth-Century Fiction,* 16 (1961-62), 177-79.

Carlisle, Janice. "The Face in the Mirror: *Villette* and the Conventions of Autobiography." *ELH,* 46 (1979), 262-89.

Carlyle, Thomas. "Biography." In *Critical and Miscellaneous Essays.* London: Chapman and Hall, 1888. Vol. II, 36-48.

Cecil, David. *Early Victorian Novelists: Essays in Revaluation.* London: Constable, 1934, pp. 109-44.

Chase, Richard. "The Brontës, or, Myth Domesticated." In *Forms of Modern Fiction.* Ed. William Van O'Connor. Bloomington: Indiana Univ. Press, 1948.

Cockshut, A. O. J. *Truth to Life: The Art of Biography in the Nineteenth Century.* New York: Harcourt Brace Jovanovich, 1974.

Colby, Robert A. "*Villette* and the Life of the Mind." *PMLA,* 75 (1960), 410-19.

Craik, W. A. *The Brontë Novels.* London: Methuen, 1968.

Cruttwell, Patrick, "Makers and Persons." *Hudson Review,* 12 (1959-60), 487-507.

Day, Martin S. "Central Concepts of *Jane Eyre.*" *Personalist,* 41 (1960), 495-505.

Dessner, Lawrence Jay. *The Homely Web of Truth: A Study of Charlotte Brontë's Novels.* The Hague: Mouton, 1975.

Dinnage, Rosemary. "Re-creating Eve." Rev. of *The Madwoman in the Attic: The Woman Writer and the Nineteenth-Century Literary Imagination,* by Sandra M. Gilbert and Susan Gubar. *The New York Review of Books,* 26, No. 20 (1979), 6-8.

Drabble, Margaret. "The Writer as Recluse: The Theme of Solitude in the Works of the Brontës." *Brontë Society Transactions,* 16, No. 4 (1974), 259-69.

Dunbar, Georgia. "Proper Names in *Villette.*" *Nineteenth-Century Fiction,* 15 (1960), 77-80.

Eagleton, Terry. *Myths of Power: A Marxist Study of the Brontës.* New York: Barnes and Noble, 1975.

Edel, Leon. *Literary Biography.* Toronto: Univ. of Toronto Press, 1957.

Eliot, T. S. *The Three Voices of Poetry.* London: Cambridge Univ. Press, 1953.

Ericksen, Donald H. "Imagery as Structure in *Jane Eyre.*" *Victorian Newsletter,* No. 30 (1966), pp. 18-24.

Erikson, Erik Homburger. "The Problem of Ego Identity." *Journal of the American Psychoanalytic Association,* 4, No. 1 (1956), 56-121.

Ewbank, Inga-Stina. *Their Proper Sphere: A Study of the Brontë Sisters as Early-Victorian Female Novelists.* London: Edward Arnold, 1966.

Flahiff, F. T. C. "Formative Ideas in the Novels of Charlotte and Emily Brontë." Diss. Univ. of Toronto, 1965.

Friedman, Norman. "Point of View in Fiction: The Development of a Critical Concept." *PMLA,* 70 (1955), 1160-84.

Garraty, John A. *The Nature of Biography.* London: Jonathan Cape, 1957.

Gaskell, Elizabeth. *The Life of Charlotte Brontë.* Ed. Alan Shelston. Harmondsworth, England: Penguin, 1975.

Gates, Barbara. "'Visionary Woe' and Its Revision: Another Look at Jane Eyre's Pictures." *Ariel,* 7, No. 4 (1976), 36-49.

Gérin, Winifred. *Charlotte Brontë: The Evolution of Genius.* Oxford: Clarendon, 1967.

Gilbert, Sandra M., and Susan Gubar. *The Madwoman in the Attic: The Woman Writer and the Nineteenth-Century Literary Imagination.* New Haven: Yale Univ. Press, 1979.

Halloran, Margaret Anne. "The Apocalypse of Charlotte Brontë." Unpublished paper.

Heilman, Robert B. "Charlotte Brontë, Reason, and the Moon." *Nineteenth-Century Fiction,* 14 (1959-60), 283-302.

———. "Charlotte Brontë's 'New' Gothic." In *Victorian Literature: Modern Essays in Criticism.* Ed. Austin Wright. New York: Oxford Univ. Press, 1961, pp. 71-85.

Hook, Andrew D. "Charlotte Brontë, the Imagination, and *Villette.*" In *The Brontës: A Collection of Critical Essays.* Ed. Ian Gregor. Englewood Cliffs, N.J.: Prentice-Hall, 1970, pp. 137-56.

James, Henry. "The Lesson of Balzac." In *The Future of the Novel: Essays on the Art of Fiction.* Ed. Leon Edel. New York: Vintage Books, 1956, pp. 97-124.

Johnson, E. D. H. "'Daring the Dread Glance': Charlotte Brontë's Treatment of the Supernatural in *Villette.*" *Nineteenth-Century Fiction,* 20, No. 4 (1966), 325-36.

Karl, Frederick R. "The Brontës: The Self Defined, Redefined, and Refined." In *The Victorian Experience: The Novelists.* Ed. Richard A. Levine. Athens: Ohio Univ. Press, 1976, pp. 121-50.

Keefe, Robert. *Charlotte Brontë's World of Death.* Austin: Univ. of Texas Press, 1979.

Kinkead-Weekes, Mark. "The Place of Love in *Jane Eyre* and *Wuthering Heights.*" In *The Brontës: A Collection of Critical Essays.* Ed. Ian Gregor. Englewood Cliffs, N.J.: Prentice-Hall, 1970, pp. 76-95.

Knies, Earl A. *The Art of Charlotte Brontë.* Athens: Ohio Univ. Press, 1969.

Kris, Ernst. "The Personal Myth: A Problem in Psychoanalytic Technique." *Journal of the American Psychoanalytic Association,* 4, No. 4 (1956), 653-81.

Langer, Susanne K. "The Great Literary Forms." In her *Feeling and Form: A Theory of Art.* New York: Charles Scribner's Sons, 1953.

Langford, Thomas. "The Three Pictures in *Jane Eyre.*" *Victorian Newsletter,* No. 31 (1967), pp. 47-48.

Linder, Cynthia A. *Romantic Imagery in the Novels of Charlotte Brontë.* London: Macmillan, 1978.

Locke, John. "Of retention." In *An Essay Concerning Human Understanding.* Ed. Raymond Wilburn. Everyman's Library. London: Dent, 1947.

Lodge, David. "Fire and Eyre: Charlotte Brontë's War of Earthly Elements." In *The Brontës: A Collection of Critical Essays.* Ed. Ian Gregor. Englewood Cliffs, N.J.: Prentice-Hall, 1970, pp. 110-36.

Martin, Robert Bernard. *The Accents of Persuasion.* London: Faber and Faber, 1966.

Maurois, André. *Aspects of Biography.* New York: Frederick Ungar, 1929.

Millett, Kate. *Sexual Politics.* New York: Avon, 1969, pp. 191-202 (on *Villette*).

Millgate, Jane. "Narrative Distance in *Jane Eyre*: The Relevance of the Pictures." *Modern Language Review,* 63 (1968), 315-19.

Moglen, Helene. *Charlotte Brontë: The Self Conceived.* New York: Norton, 1976.

Morris, John N. *Versions of the Self.* New York: Basic Books, 1966.

Moser, Lawrence E., S.J. "From Portrait to Person: A Note on the Surrealistic in *Jane Eyre.*" *Nineteenth-Century Fiction,* 20 (1965-66), 275-81.

Nicolson, Harold. *The Development of English Biography.* London: The Hogarth Press, 1927.

Olney, James. *Metaphors of Self: The Meaning of Autobiography.* Princeton: Princeton Univ. Press, 1972.

Pascal, Roy. "The Autobiographical Novel and The Autobiography." *Essays in Criticism,* 9 (1959), 134-50.

———. *Design and Truth in Autobiography.* London: Routledge and Kegan Paul, 1960.

Peters, Margot. *Unquiet Soul: A Biography of Charlotte Brontë.* Garden City, New York: Doubleday, 1975.

Pinion, F. B. *A Brontë Companion.* London: Macmillan, 1975.

Reed, Joseph W., Jr. *English Biography in the Early Nineteenth Century 1801-1838.* New Haven: Yale Univ. Press, 1966.

Rinehart, Keith. "The Victorian Approach to Autobiography." *Modern Philology,* 51 (1954), 177-86.

Scargill, M. H. "'All Passion Spent': A Revaluation of *Jane Eyre.*" *University of Toronto Quarterly,* 19 (1949-50), 120-25.

Shannon, Edgar F., Jr. "The Present Tense in *Jane Eyre.*" *Nineteenth-Century Fiction,* 10 (1955-56), 141-45.

Shumaker, Wayne. *English Autobiography: Its Emergence, Materials, and Form.* Berkeley: Univ. of California Press, 1954.

Stephen, Leslie. "Autobiography." In his *Hours in a Library.* Rev. ed. London: Smith, Elder and Co., 1892. Vol. III, 237-70.

———. "Charlotte Brontë." In his *Hours in a Library.* Rev. ed. London: Smith, Elder and Co., 1892. Vol. III, 1-30.

Tanner, Tony, introd. *Villette.* By Charlotte Brontë. Ed. Mark Lilly. Penguin English Library. Harmondsworth, England: Penguin, 1979.

Tillotson, Kathleen. *Novels of the Eighteen-Forties.* London: Oxford Univ. Press, 1961.

Tompkins, J. M. S. "Jane Eyre's 'Iron Shroud.'" *Modern Language Review,* 22 (1927), 195-97.

Traversi, Derek. "The Brontë Sisters and *Wuthering Heights.*" In *From Dickens to Hardy.* Vol. VI of *Pelican Guide to English Literature.* Ed. Boris Ford. Harmondsworth, England: Penguin, 1958, pp. 256-73.

Watson, Melvin R. "Form and Substance in the Brontë Novels." In *From Jane Austen to Joseph Conrad.* Ed. Robert C. Rathburn and Martin Steinmann, Jr. Minneapolis: Univ. of Minnesota Press, 1958, pp. 106-17.

Winnifrith, Tom. *The Brontës.* New York: Collier-Macmillan, 1977.

———. *The Brontës and Their Background.* New York: Barnes and Noble, 1973.

www.ingramcontent.com/pod-product-compliance
Lightning Source LLC
Chambersburg PA
CBHW072042040426
42447CB00012BB/2971